IT HURTS TO HEAL

Also by John Huggett:

Six Keys to Healing

It Hurts to Heal

The story of

JOHN AND CHRISTINE HUGGETT

as told by Christine Huggett

KINGSWAY PUBLICATIONS

EASTBOURNE

First published 1984
Second edition 1988

Biblical quotations are from the
Revised Standard Version, copyrighted 1946, 1952
© 1971, 1973 by the Division of Christian Education of the
National Council of the Churches of
Christ in the USA.

*Many names in this book have been changed
in the interests of confidentiality.*

British Library Cataloguing in Publication Data

Huggett, Christine
It hurts to heal.—2nd ed.
1. Christian church. Ministry
I. Title
262'.14

ISBN 0 86065 644 6

KINGSWAY PUBLICATIONS LTD
Lottbridge Drove, Eastbourne, E. Sussex BN23 6NT
Typeset by Nuprint Ltd, Harpenden, Herts AL5 4SE.
Printed and bound in Great Britain
by Collins, Glasgow.

This book is dedicated to
the memory of
Vivien, Linda, Paul Seal, and *Rosemary*

Contents

Introduction

A question that we are frequently asked is, 'How did you come to be doing your healing ministry?'

This book is an attempt to answer that question. The story, which spans twenty-three years, tells in particular of the pain and suffering which helped to prepare us for our faith ministry, and of the first stages in the subsequent development of our work. Although the account is seen through the eyes of Christine, we have written it together.

God leads and trains people in a variety of ways, but our own experience has been that 'it hurts to heal'.

CHRIS AND JOHN HUGGETT

I

A Sister's Grief

John and I were waiting at a bus stop in Tonbridge High Street that hot sticky day in July. The middle-aged man who was about to break the news to me was standing at the front of the queue. His mind was in a conflict.

'Should I say something to her or not? Does she already know?'

I knew Mr Denton quite well, so was not surprised when he approached me. But I wondered why he looked so hesitant.

'Have you seen your parents today, Christine?' he asked.

'What a funny question!' I thought. The noise of the bus swinging in by the kerb almost drowned my reply.

'No...but I saw them last night. They brought our wedding present over to my flat.'

'Well, I'm afraid your sister Vivien passed away last night.'

'I'm sorry,' I stuttered, 'I don't understand.'

'Your sister Vivien *died* last night.'

John put his arm around me and we stood there stunned while others boarded the bus. Vivien, aged fourteen, was one of my five sisters. There had been nothing wrong with her. She was a healthy bouncing teenager and going to be a bridesmaid at our wedding in a month's time. We had already seen her in her blue brocade dress and white shoes. How could she be dead?

We climbed on the bus in a daze. The short journey of three miles to Southborough seemed endless. So did the walk to my parents' council house. Whatever could have happened since the previous night? Only a few hours ago we had been laughing and making plans with my mother and father. But there was no laughter now, only the sound of muffled sobs could be heard as we entered the lounge.

The family were sitting around lifelessly, looking rather like rag dolls.

'What happened?' I cried, as I hugged first one and then another.

Gradually the story emerged. The previous evening Vivien had been at the local youth club just along the road. She was doing gymnastics on a mattress when she collapsed. Thinking that she had fainted, the people in charge put her outside on a chair. After a while they realized that something was wrong, and she was rushed to Pembury Hospital. But she was found to be dead on arrival. When my parents walked into the hospital later that night they were told bluntly, 'Your daughter is dead.'

As John and I listened to this account we were soon shedding tears with the others. My mother kept saying, 'Why has she been taken? She never harmed anybody. Where is she now? Please tell me, where is she?' Gently we tried to calm her.

'I can't understand it,' she went on. 'The doctor can't help either. He's looked up her medical records and apart from the usual childhood complaints she's never been ill.'

It certainly was a mystery. The local newspaper was quick to catch on to the story. They made it front page news. It was an odd experience to go out and read on the placards, 'Girl dies at Youth Club'.

Every day we waited anxiously for news. A policeman called regularly, but always to report that he could tell us nothing. A week dragged by making it only three weeks to our wedding. Should we postpone it? It seemed selfish to be even thinking of our marriage at such a time. And yet everything had already been arranged. We were moving to Bristol, where John had a place at theological college. We had rented a flat there and the removal van was booked.

'We'll postpone the wedding if you want us to, Mum,' I suggested tentatively.

'No, don't!' came back the instant reply. 'Go ahead as you've planned. Whenever you get married I shall still see her standing there in her bridesmaid's dress.'

At last the policeman brought some news.

'Acute myocarditis is what she died of,' he announced. Very rare in a young person, the doctors say. They had to call in a top pathologist for a second opinion. That's why it's been so long.'

We felt relieved that we could now go ahead with the funeral arrangements. But we were full of unanswered questions.

As time went on we learned that acute myocarditis is acute inflammation of the muscular tissue of the heart. A doctor told me, 'It's a condition, not a disease, and cannot be inherited. The chances of this happening again in the same family are one in a million.' We all felt reassured. It was a blessing that we could not see into the future.

Vivien was buried a fortnight after she died. We wondered how the whole episode would affect our life together. Perhaps, because we were moving away to a new area, it would soon fade into the background. Those we left behind were the ones who would really miss her.

The next two years were spent in Bristol, during which time our first son Stephen was born. After that we moved to Hailsham, a small market town in Sussex. It was there that John served his first curacy. When we arrived we were given a very warm welcome and found that our larder was stacked high with food! The parishioners really took us to their hearts, especially one year old Stephen, whom they thoroughly spoilt. From the start we felt at home and slipped easily into our roles of curate and wife.

The parish is far flung. The lovely ancient church with its square tower stands in the centre of the town. In the country a few miles out you will find the little daughter church of St Mark's, Magham Down. On the outskirts of Hailsham is an expanding residential area where Hawkswood Church

13

Hall helps to serve the community.

The vicar and his wife were elderly, and he had been there for thirty-six years. Just as we had been warned, we soon had an interregnum to cope with. And John kept the three churches going for seven months, which included a Christmas and an Easter.

So it was a very busy period. We had meetings each night and often they were held in our home. On Easter Day John clocked up a grand total of eight services. And at lunchtime that day the curate was to be seen sitting in the churchyard, still fully robed, munching his sandwiches! But we were happy. And while we were at Hailsham our second son, Paul, was born, much to the delight of everyone.

Our happiness was short-lived.

I come from a large family. There were eight of us children, six girls and two boys. I was the eldest. They say that you should not have favourites, but you do. There is always one with whom you feel an affinity. In my case it was my youngest sister Linda and she often used to come and stay with us at Hailsham. At thirteen she was tall and well built, with long brown hair—a typical lively teenager.

By the time that the new vicar arrived we were ready for a holiday. So we decided to stay with my parents at Southborough and bring Linda back home with us afterwards.

My family were delighted to see us again. They didn't at all mind acting as babysitters. Neither did John when one day I decided to go swimming. Three of my sisters agreed to come with me: Janet, Margaret and Linda.

It's strange how you remember the little things afterwards. 'I'll pay the bus fares,' I said casually. 'Somebody else can treat me on the way back.' We didn't know then that we should not be coming back by bus.

We enjoyed our swim, but the water was cold so three of us decided to get out. Linda wanted to stay in longer.

'I'll be out in a minute!' she shouted, laughing up at us from the water.

We bounded up the stairs to the spectators' gallery. From

14

there we had a good view of the swimmers and we settled down to watch and munch crisps. Suddenly I shot out of my seat, nearly choking.

'What's the matter?' my sisters asked.

'It's Linda!' I gasped. There was her lifeless body floating on the water. We raced down the stairs, our hearts in our mouths.

By the time that we reached the pool Linda had been dragged to the side. She lay there stretched out on her stomach, her head to one side, blue in the face and foaming at the mouth. My sister Margaret took one look at her and said softly, 'It's the same as Vivien.'

'Oh no,' I thought, 'not Linda, my darling Linda!' The attendants were giving her artificial respiration.

'Call an ambulance quickly!' we pleaded. 'You must listen to us. We know it's not drowning. Please get her to a hospital.'

The man looked at us pityingly. We were standing huddled together, shivering and shaking from head to toe.

'Make them some tea,' he ordered. They gave it to us. It was hot and sickly sweet.

The ambulance arrived, its siren wailing.

'Thank goodness that the Kent and Sussex Hospital is fairly close!' I thought anxiously. 'Perhaps if we get her there quickly they can save her.'

We sat opposite her in the ambulance, still huddled together. I sat in the centre with an arm around each sister. Both were sobbing. We watched while the ambulance men administered oxygen. I cried out, 'Please, God, don't let her die!'

At the hospital we were greeted by Ruth, a Christian nurse whom we knew. How strange that she should be on duty, and what a comfort she was! She took me in her arms.

'I'm sorry, Christine, but I don't think she's going to make it.'

I stared at her disbelievingly.

We were ushered into a little room to wait and given some more tea.

'Your parents are on their way,' Ruth told us. Our thoughts

turned to them. How would this affect them? They soon arrived, white-faced and shaken. Just four years ago almost to the day they had lived through a similar ordeal.

'How many doctors are with her, Ruth?' my mother asked.

'About ten,' she replied.

We sat waiting in silence. The minutes ticked by until about an hour had passed. All this time I had been praying desperately, but suddenly I just knew Linda was dead. They had given up trying and so I gave up praying. It was all over.

Shortly afterwards a doctor opened the door and stood there for a moment. Then he said sadly, 'We did all we could.'

'Thank you,' my mother said quietly. 'We're sure you did.'

We piled into my father's car and in a daze made for my parents' home. John was standing anxiously at the front door.

'It's the same as Vivien, John,' my mother said, her voice expressionless. My husband's eyes met mine. In that moment we shared our grief and the total disbelief that this could be happening.

It's difficult to describe the days that followed. One of the worst experiences was waking up in the morning. Although sleep itself provided a relief, those first moments were horrific as the awareness of what had happened gradually dawned upon me.

Shock is strange: we are protected by the chemistry of our bodies from feeling its full impact all at once. First, there is a feeling of acute weakness. Then one is plunged into a sort of twilight existence where everything is unreal. I found myself drifting backwards and forwards, from hopes that it was a dream to the harsh reality that it was not.

Only some time later did the full shock of Linda's death hit me. John and I were at Tunbridge Wells in British Home Stores. We were sitting in the restaurant enjoying a cup of coffee when I turned to him and exclaimed, 'Why are all these people going about their normal lives as though nothing has happened?' I felt that life for me could never be the same again.

The diagnosis for Linda was identical to that of Vivien: acute myocarditis. It was no comfort that it was such a rare thing to happen twice in one family. Which one of us was it going to strike next? We were all worried. The doctor advised the whole family to have checkups, though it was difficult to see how these could help if the condition could not be detected beforehand.

We returned to Hailsham with heavy hearts.

'It's funny,' I said to John on the way, 'but I never got around to making up Linda's bed before we left.'

The shock began to wear off and the real grief set in. This revealed itself in a variety of ways. Each Wednesday we held a service in one of the local old people's homes. The old folk would gather in the day room for a good sing and then John would give a short talk. Afterwards we would chat with them individually. One afternoon I was listening to John and looking at the well-worn pathetic faces in front of me when suddenly I found that I was resenting those senior citizens for being alive! Some were slumped motionless in their wheel-chairs, others were fumbling with their hearing aids and one or two were muttering incoherently.

'How is it that old people like this can be allowed to live so long?' I thought despairingly. It didn't make sense. I felt they had outlived their allotted time of threescore years and ten. 'If God had to take somebody, why not them? Why should they be left when my young and healthy sisters have died?' I asked. Then of course I began to feel guilty for thinking such things.

I experienced guilt on another occasion, too. As the time passes you imagine that you are getting over your grief, then all of a sudden you are caught unawares. I was in the supermarket one afternoon and happened to notice the tins of mandarin oranges. I found myself sobbing inside, almost uncontrollably. My mind went back to when Linda had stayed with us last. She had come shopping with me to that same supermarket.

'May we have some mandarin oranges for tea?' she had asked.

'No,' I'd replied flatly, 'we'll have pineapple instead. It's cheaper.'

'If only she were here now!' I thought wistfully. 'I would give her plates and plates full of mandarin oranges!' How I wished that I had bought them then! It seemed so ridiculous, looking back on it. I had denied her what she fancied for the sake of a few pence. My sense of guilt was, however, out of all proportion.

I longed to find relief from my inner turmoil, but there was none.

Not even my faith in God helped me. As a child I had asked Jesus into my life and I believe that he had come in by his Holy Spirit. But where was he now? I certainly couldn't feel him any more. Had he gone? After Vivien's death I had felt his peace, but this time there was no peace, just pain. I wondered whether God was real. It suddenly became imperative for me to know.

'God, are you still there?' I asked. I could sense no answer.

We soon moved to another parish, in Worthing. It was lovely to live just five minutes' walk from the sea, especially in the summer. But during the long dark winter evenings the wind would whistle through the big bay windows and I would sit alone in our spacious lounge. I began to cry out to God even more earnestly.

'I believe you are there, but it's not enough any more just to believe. I must know!' I was married to a clergyman and sharing our faith in Jesus was our life. Although I was very much in love with John I couldn't see how I could continue to be married to him unless somehow God answered my prayer.

The weeks and months sped by and John was unaware of the inner struggle that I was undergoing. We had a record of Ernest Lough singing that lovely aria from Handel's *Messiah*, 'I know that my Redeemer liveth'. When John was out I would play it over and over again. 'Please, God, I want to *know* that my Redeemer liveth,' I constantly pleaded.

Two years passed and I was still asking God.

It was the Christmas market at church and the large hall was decorated for the festive season. A tall Christmas tree

18

stood in the far corner. We pushed our way through the crowds so that Stephen and Paul could join the queue for Santa Claus. I left John to keep a watchful eye on the boys while I had a look around.

Among the stalls there was one piled high with second-hand books. As I rummaged through them one caught my eye. It was a paperback written by Oral Roberts and entitled, *The Baptism with the Holy Spirit and the Value of Speaking in Tongues Today*. I bought it for just a few pence.

That evening after John went out I put the boys to bed and settled down in the lounge to read my book. I lay stretched out on the rug in front of the fire. As I read I became more and more intrigued.

The author was relating the story of the Day of Pentecost. 'Christians today need a personal Pentecost for themselves,' he wrote. 'The baptism in the Holy Spirit is still available and is happening to many Christians all over the world. This experience is one of the secrets of the effectiveness of the early church.'

I wondered whether this could be true. I had learnt a lot through belonging to the Open Brethren; they are great Bible teachers. But they had never taught me anything about this and neither had the Church of England. So I began to ask the Lord about it.

'Is this true, what this book says, Lord? Can people still be baptized in the Holy Spirit today?'

I was quite unprepared for what followed. It was an experience which I consider to be one of the most beautiful in my life.

As I was speaking, God descended upon me. The movement started deep inside my stomach. It reminded me of when I was pregnant. It was as real and as vibrant as an unborn child moving around inside me. But it was fluid, and seemed to flow. I could feel it rising slowly upwards. It was warm and I wanted to yield to it. I felt excited at the reality of it all. Jesus was with me and my ache for him was being satisfied.

Gradually the movement surged up through my body and

out of my mouth. Although I had been speaking in English, I found the words changing into another language. I was speaking in a tongue. I understood then why the Authorized Version of the Bible says, 'Out of his belly shall flow rivers of living water' (John 7:38). That is just what was happening to me.

I sat there cocooned in the powerful presence of Jesus. At last, after two years, I could say, 'I *know*.' I still didn't understand why my sisters had died. But now that I knew that Jesus was alive it didn't seem quite so important. They were in his hands.

Of one thing I was sure. God himself had visited me in no uncertain manner. He had seen the longing in my heart and the persistence with which I had sought him. My desperate prayer had been answered and I would never again doubt that he was real.

But whatever was John going to say when he came in?

2

The Proud Curate

For John it had been just like any other Saturday night. He had been leading the church youth club in their usual games and epilogue. How could he have guessed that something was happening to me which would alter the course of our lives?

By the time that he left the club that chilly December evening it was getting late. He was glad to jump in the car and drive the few hundred yards home. As he drew up outside he noticed that the lounge light was on.

'Good,' he thought, 'Chris is still up.'

'I'm back, darling,' he called as he unlocked the front door, 'thanks for waiting up for me.'

I greeted him with a huge hug.

'I've something to tell you,' I said to him excitedly.

'Oh, what's that?' he asked, taking off his overcoat and scarf.

'I've just had a dynamic experience of Jesus. He's baptized me in the Holy Spirit and I spoke in tongues.'

John smiled at me shyly. 'I am pleased,' he murmured.

He didn't know quite what to say. John was constantly arriving home to find me unhappy. This was not surprising in the circumstances. We were in a very large parish of twenty-six thousand people and my husband was curate to a vicar who was often ill. This meant additional work for John, so he was always out. There was the hospital chaplaincy to assist with, meetings of various kinds to attend, an unending list of people to visit and the responsibility of his own daughter church.

Meanwhile, I was left at home. I felt imprisoned in the house with our two small boys. I would have loved more Christian fellowship but it was hard to get babysitters.

We were also desperately short of money. Part of John's stipend had to go towards his expenses. The church didn't cover these adequately, so we found that our food money could end up being spent on petrol for the parish!

Once we literally had nothing to eat and the most amazing thing happened. I was stopped by a lady outside a shop and offered some cakes that she had just bought. Another time I found some money lying in the gutter.

My friend joked about this. 'Have you been praying again?' she laughed.

But my deepest unhappiness was the heartache following Linda's death. I remember one day being in tears when John came home.

'Don't you cry as well!' he snapped impatiently. 'I've already had three women crying on my shoulder today!'

It was not that John didn't care. It was just that the work that he was doing totally drained him. He longed to see me happier and more at peace.

So on that particular Saturday night he was relieved to find me so contented.

'The question is now,' he wondered, 'will it last?' But as we went upstairs his mind quickly moved on to his next day's sermons.

In the next few days John could see that there was something different about me. But what was it? He just could not put his finger on it. There was a calmness, a serenity. He was genuinely pleased for me—though the thought never occurred to him that he might benefit from a similar experience. Even if it had done he would have had no opportunity to stop and think about it. Events were always overtaking him.

As we were eating our lunch one day a knock came at the door.

'Good afternoon, Mr Huggett.' The man who spoke was dressed entirely in black, and we recognized him as one of the local funeral directors.

'Did you want to see me?' John enquired.

'The cremation starts in twenty minutes, Reverend,' he said, glancing at John's casual clothes and at the unfinished meal on the table.

'Cremation...you mean...oh no, not again!' This was not the first time that the vicar had arranged for John to take a funeral and had forgotten to tell him.

'I'll have to move fast!' my husband said.

I managed to find his black shoes while he scrambled into his clerical robes, snatched his Bible and service book, and ran out of the door. I heard him start the car and he was off.

There was no sign of the hearse or the mourners' cars ahead of him. Somehow he would have to catch them up and overtake them. Normally John would need to be at the crematorium in good time before they arrived, and it was five miles from our home.

'Who's died?' he wondered, pushing his foot down hard on the accelerator. 'And what on earth am I going to say at the service?'

He kept straining to see if he could spot the funeral cars, but as he passed through Findon Valley there was still no sign of them. At last he saw them, just before the turning into the crematorium grounds.

'I wonder what the mourners are thinking now?' he reflected, as he shot past the procession and pulled into the drive just in front of the hearse. Before the service began he was given the name of the deceased and no one appeared to realize that John knew nothing of the person's background.

Life certainly was hectic for my husband. He seemed caught up in a frenzy of activity. He had no regular meal times and it became difficult to get a complete day off each week. I felt that John neglected me and the children and that we were given second place to 'the work'. Outwardly he appeared dignified and unruffled. Inwardly he felt frustrated—though he was not the sort to complain.

I was in the kitchen one morning peeling potatoes when the telephone rang. I answered it.

'Please would you tell your husband to call and collect a sponge cake for tomorrow's coffee morning?' the female voice demanded and gave an address. Later I passed the message on to John.

'Right,' he said with a sigh. 'I'll have to take the extra chairs to the hall first. After that I must get the choir robes to the laundry. Then I'll collect the sponge on the way back.'

My heart sank. 'After all the years John has spent training for the ministry,' I thought, 'he's become an errand boy! Surely all that preparation was for more than this.'

It was true that his sermons were appreciated. Some of his congregation had expressed a wish to hire the Royal Albert Hall so that everyone could hear him preach! But a lot of the work that he was doing was trivial and could be done just as well by somebody untrained.

The next day we were sitting at the breakfast table opening our mail.

'What a cheek!' John exclaimed suddenly. 'Take a look at this!' He handed me a letter.

'Dear John and Chris, something wonderful has happened to me and I just had to let you know. I have been baptized in the Holy Spirit and am speaking in tongues.'

The letter from John's younger brother was postmarked Hull where Christopher was at university. It was very seldom that he wrote to us and now here was a lengthy letter all about 'tongues', or so it seemed to John.

Christopher wrote, 'A number at university speak in tongues. It was normal for Christians in the New Testament and I believe it's normal for all Christians today.'

My husband was furious, 'I don't see how "tongues" can be for all Christians. Doesn't the Bible say, "Do *all* speak with tongues?" That must indicate that some Christians don't. I don't need this gift. After all, I'm a minister!'

John was quite adamant about this. It was only later that he realized that when Paul asked that question he was referring to tongues in church, where they need interpreting.

But in his pride John had closed his mind to a much more profound truth, for release in the Holy Spirit and speaking in tongues are often the gateway into a new dimension of Christian living. He was unaware of his need. Little did he know what awaited him in our next parish.

The vicar of a parish at Wunford in Surrey had been looking for a curate to take charge of two daughter churches. When we journeyed to look over this parish we were surprised to find that the vicar and his wife wanted to interview both of us. The vicar's wife asked me questions while the vicar interviewed John. Then both of them interrogated both of us. We were obviously being very closely observed to see whether we were suitable. We found out that this happened with two other couples as well.

This particular vicar felt it necessary to know all that was going on in his parish and each activity had to slot into its appropriate compartment. I was asked if I spoke in tongues and had to promise that I would keep to myself the fact that I did. John was asked the same question and his definite reply in the negative satisfied the vicar.

We were very attracted to the place so it was a great day when the letter arrived to say that John had been chosen for the post.

Our first year in Wunford was really happy. The strains upon our marriage were greatly reduced. John still had a very busy programme but everything was highly organized. The vicar encouraged him to have proper meal breaks, to stop working if possible by nine-thirty each evening, and to regard his day off as sacrosanct. We became more of a family again, which brought us closer.

We spent a lovely holiday together on the Isle of Wight. The boys' favourite haunt there was Blackgang Chine on the cliff top. They loved the winding pathways filled with gnomes and the model village. At six years Stephen was able to climb right inside the large army tanks in the adventure playground, while his three year old brother preferred the crooked house and the hall of mirrors. They both enjoyed the smugglers' cave. At night the Chine illuminations are an impressive spectacle and can be seen for miles.

It was while we were at Blackgang Chine one evening that I found that I could not breathe properly. We were walking up the cliff at the time, enjoying the scenery, when I seemed to run out of breath. My legs became heavy and I felt that I couldn't take another step. I panicked, convinced that I was about to meet a fate similar to that of my two sisters. Somehow John helped me to the car and we got back to our hotel. A doctor was sent for and he came very quickly. After examining me he stated, 'Your problem is stress.'

I looked at him blankly. 'But I'm not under any stress,' I said, 'and haven't been for some time. I'm very happy.'

'Yes,' he replied kindly, 'but that is when your body reacts to stress, not while you're undergoing it. Sometimes the outward physical symptoms appear a long time afterwards. You're suffering as a result of stress in your past.'

In the future we would find ourselves ministering to many people with physical problems of which the root cause was stress. The Holy Spirit shows us when this is so and we point it out to the person concerned. We often encounter the same blank look that I must have given that doctor. We are then able to explain the way our body works. It's a question of reaping what we sow. We may think that we have come through a traumatic time extremely well, but usually it will eventually take its toll on our bodies.

What happened to me did not mar our holiday and we all returned to Wunford much refreshed.

As summer gave way to autumn one other thing slightly unsettled me. I began to have an occasional sense of foreboding about our son Paul. I felt sure that something was going to happen to him. I tried to brush this aside, telling myself that it was due to the shocks which I had suffered. But the feeling persisted.

Our lounge in Wunford was small and cosy. The red velvet curtains which hung at the French windows added an extra touch of warmth to the room. I spent a lot of time there, especially in the evenings while John was out. One night as I was praying I heard a quiet voice speaking in my mind.

26

'Stretch out your hands.'

I obeyed almost automatically and as I did my hands began to vibrate and burn. I had never heard the voice before but I felt that it was the Lord and I was filled with a sense of awe.

'I will use your hands to bless millions.' The words came distinctly and with authority. I wondered what it could mean. I didn't connect it with the laying on of hands because I had never seen this, except at confirmation services.

When John returned from his meeting I tried to explain my experience to him. He laughed disbelievingly.

'The Lord uses everyone's hands. And the word "millions" must be wrong. Perhaps it was "many",' he added.

I felt hurt: I knew what I had heard. I decided to store it away—one day in the future it might make sense. So I told no one. We had few really close friends who would understand anyway.

There were some, though, who were used to such 'supernatural' happenings. Our friends Mark and Karen lived near the community centre where Paul attended a playgroup. We often called to see them on our way to collect him. Mark worked for a Christian publishing firm, and they were members of Wunford Baptist Church. We were both intrigued by some of the 'strange goings-on' at that church.

'People are being healed through prayer,' they said 'and are speaking in tongues.'

John couldn't seem to escape from this! It was everywhere. In the churches, in the ministers' meetings, wherever he went the topic of conversation was the work of the Holy Spirit. Our vicar, though, was the odd one out. He seemed to be unsympathetic to anything 'charismatic'.

'Have you read *The Holy Spirit and You* by Dennis and Rita Bennett?' Mark asked John one morning as he brought in some books from his car.

'No, I haven't,' John replied warily.

'You must. It deals with the sort of questions you're asking about the gifts of the Spirit. I'll get it for you.'

We collected Paul and made our way back home.

'What I don't agree with is calling it the *baptism* of the Holy Spirit,' John said to me as we passed the local supermarket. 'The Bible speaks of only one baptism. Surely that would make two! And why do I need to *receive* the Holy Spirit again? I received him when I became a Christian.'

I felt concerned for my husband.

'I wish I could answer your theological questions, darling. I only know what a difference it's made to me.'

We entered the house and John put the kettle on for a cup of tea.

'The Bible says that God gives certain gifts to certain people,' he continued. '*I* have the gift of preaching.' His pride almost lit up his clerical collar. 'If God wants to give me any other gifts he will.' The subject was closed.

One May morning soon afterwards John and I, together with three others, travelled as delegates from our parish to a conference entitled 'Strategy for Evangelism'. It was held at Pontin's Holiday Camp, Morecambe, and was attended by nine hundred Christians from all denominations.

At one of the morning Bible readings the passage included John 14:12: 'Truly, truly, I say to you, he who believes in me will also do the works that I do; and greater works than these will he do, because I go to the Father.'

The speaker said that this referred to the spread of the gospel throughout the world once Jesus had ascended. I couldn't believe my ears. I leaned over to John. 'Whatever is he talking about?' I said. 'It means more than that!'

We thought no more of it until the last day of the conference. At the final meeting, a Communion service, another speaker, who had been absent on the previous occasion, referred to the same verse. His interpretation of it was very different.

'This promise has just recently come literally true,' he announced. 'In the Indonesian Revival Christians have been turning water into wine when they had none for Holy Communion. Some have walked across water to preach the gospel to people that they could not reach otherwise. And even the dead have been raised!'

'That's more like it!' I exclaimed in a whisper. John nodded in agreement. He was beginning to ask himself whether there was a connection between this so-called baptism in the Holy Spirit and the 'greater works'. Could one of these possibly lead to the other?

After the conference John began a series of six sermons on the Holy Spirit. When he was due to speak on 'The Fullness of the Holy Spirit', he said to himself 'I shall avoid anything controversial, like tongues or Holy Spirit baptism. I'll concentrate on the need to be filled continually.' But God had other ideas!

The book that Mark had promised John, *The Holy Spirit and You*, was passed on to me. I read it avidly and just could not wait for John to read it as well. So I put it on his bedside table.

As we climbed into bed that night he picked it up and started reading. I pretended not to notice and turned the other way, praying desperately that the book would be able to help him where I could not.

As John read, the answers to what had puzzled him for so long began to fall into place. He could see that there were several baptisms in the New Testament. The book quoted scriptures which satisfied him on that point. As for receiving the Holy Spirit, he realized that it didn't mean a second conversion but a release of power.

Suddenly he turned to me. 'I want this!' he said with conviction. My heart leapt. At last he understood.

So on the Saturday morning, just eighteen months after my Pentecost, John shut himself in our lounge to be alone with the Lord. A few minutes later I heard him calling me.

'I've asked for it and nothing's happened!' he said indignantly.

I laughed, amused at his annoyance. 'Ask again, then!' I said.

But now the fears were coming fast. 'What if it isn't God who answers me?' he queried. 'How will I know if it's the real thing?'

I replied simply, 'You will know.' Then I left him.

Shortly afterwards I heard a shout. 'Darling, it's happened! It's happened!'

I ran quickly to the lounge. John was full of joy and tears were in his eyes.

'Gosh, this has completely ruined tomorrow's sermon!' He smiled, his face aglow. 'I'll have to prepare it all over again.'

'Who cares?' I said, flinging my arms around him and holding him tight.

There was a slight pause.

'Somebody will when he finds out what's happened to me.' I had no need to ask who he meant.

3

Left High and Dry

John was like a child with a new toy. He just could not stop praying. For the rest of that day he disappeared upstairs at regular intervals. He had been so dry spiritually and now the living water had revived him.

'This is great!' he exclaimed as we relaxed after supper. 'I've been praying all day and I still want to pray. I feel as though I'm on cloud nine. I hope this lasts!'

'Well, I expect you'll come down to earth eventually,' I said with a smile.

At the close of Sunday evening's sermon John gave an appeal.

'If anyone here desires to be consciously filled with the Holy Spirit, please come to the vestry afterwards. We should like to pray with you.'

A tall girl in her late teens responded.

'I want what you have,' she said softly. We prayed together and soon she spoke in tongues. Then, displaying no emotion, she said, 'Thank you very much,' and was gone.

This was the first time that John had given an appeal. Nowadays the opportunity to respond to the message is a regular feature of all our meetings. It seems pointless for us to speak about Jesus still healing today without inviting people to receive his touch.

During the service I had noticed that Jennifer, a middle-aged woman, was crying. I knew that the Lord was speaking

31

to her. When we left the vestry she was still in the church, so I invited her to come round the following Tuesday afternoon.

When she arrived she confided that she had been in tears almost continually since Sunday.

'Don't worry,' I said, putting my arm around her. 'The Lord is releasing you.' We sat alone in the lounge and I laid my hands on her head, praying that Jesus would release her fully. The flood gates were immediately opened, both in tongues and tears, and I was so happy for her that I started crying as well. No wonder that John, on hearing the commotion, opened the door, took one look and promptly declared, 'I'll make a cup of tea!'

The next morning at breakfast we wondered what the vicar's attitude would be at the staff meeting.

'When we came for the interview I assured him that I didn't speak in tongues,' John recalled as he helped himself to cereal. 'But how was I to know it was going to happen to me while I was here?'

At the staff meeting that afternoon John read Acts 16:26: 'Suddenly there was a great earthquake, so that the foundations of the prison were shaken; and immediately all the doors were opened and everyone's fetters were unfastened.'

My husband then tried to explain how this verse aptly described what had happened to him and to others in the past week. The vicar said little in response and swiftly moved on to the business matters of the parish.

'What an anticlimax!' I exclaimed when John arrived home and told me. 'But it's probably not the last we've heard of it.'

That night there was a large interdenominational meeting for renewal in the town and John had been asked to lead it. He came home praising the Lord and brought in our friends Roy and Priscilla who lived opposite us. Roy was the minister of a church just along the road.

We relaxed over coffee and then began to worship the Lord. As we did, his power fell upon us and we were taken up in prayer and praise, until suddenly we realized that it was three o'clock in the morning!

We felt so strongly bound to Roy and Priscilla that we could hardly bear them to leave us. As we stood up to say goodbye our legs would not hold us and we started staggering about.

'Gosh,' I giggled, 'now I understand why they accused the disciples of being drunk on the Day of Pentecost. This is what it must have been like. We're drunk in the Spirit. At least there won't be a hangover!'

But there was, of a sort. The next morning as I entered the lounge I was hit again by the powerful presence of Jesus. I rushed upstairs to John calling, 'Darling, he's still there!'

The supernatural had become as real as the natural. But we had so much to learn in this realm. We were taught very gradually, often through our own mistakes.

Although at Morecambe we had learned from Doreen Irvine about her experiences with witchcraft, we were nowhere near ready to deal with a case of demon possession. And yet when we were asked to help a girl involved with drugs and witchcraft, we confidently travelled to her village to see her. As it happened, she was out. This was just as well because, brandishing a knife, she later attacked a group of people. Our confidence would have speedily evaporated if we had become involved.

We realized that the problem would come up again, though, so John decided to go and see Harold, a local minister who had experience in the field of deliverance. Harold was pleased to see him and gladly described some of the cases that he had encountered and the mistakes that he had made. John learned a lot from him.

As the green leaves turned to gold we were soon once again heavily involved with activities both in our parish and in other churches. Home meetings had arisen spontaneously and it was at one of these that we witnessed our first healing at close range.

Dennis, another member of Wunford Baptist Church, was particularly gifted at healing people's backs.

'People with back trouble often have one leg shorter than the other,' he explained. He asked everyone present who had troublesome backs to stretch out their legs. Sure enough in each case we could see that their legs were of unequal length. Dennis laid hands on them and prayed in the name of Jesus; we watched amazed as the shorter legs grew.

At the next staff meeting the vicar expressed his concern about the home meetings and John's involvement with them. This led to a discussion on Holy Spirit theology and there was a radical disagreement between the two.

To make matters worse, a number of church people were confused about what was happening in the area. So the vicar decided to hold a series of midweek meetings. He spoke at the first one on the traditional evangelical interpretation of Pentecost. The second week John put his 'point of view,' and the third week they both answered questions. This was not an ideal arrangement. But it did give John an opportunity to show that what was happening had a firm scriptural basis and that it was a worldwide phenomenon, not just a passing craze of the curate!

In spite of this, the vicar remained unsympathetic and eventually he warned John that it was getting difficult for them to work together. Shortly afterwards we received a list of rules from the vicar which, he made clear, applied to both of us. The primary one was that John was never in his preaching to refer to 'the baptism in the Holy Spirit, or speaking in tongues'. Other rules sought to prevent us from sharing our experiences with people in the parish. We were also forbidden to give or lend any book of a charismatic nature.

'What can we do?' I asked helplessly as we lay in bed that night talking of these latest developments. John stared at the bedroom ceiling.

'Nothing,' he answered. 'It's absolutely impossible for us to keep these rules.'

'I didn't know the vicar had the right to tell me which books I can lend,' I said indignantly. 'I'm not employed by him!'

John sat up in bed. 'We can't stem the tide,' he said slowly. 'I expect in our eagerness and enthusiasm we've made some mistakes, but we can't stop the Holy Spirit working. We can't undo the wonderful things that have happened and we certainly can't help speaking about them. I'll have to tell the vicar that we are unable to keep his rules.'

A few weeks later, on a damp, dark, wintry morning, a letter was pushed through our door. It was only a week before Christmas and we were receiving greetings cards from all our friends. We thought that perhaps it was another message of goodwill, but it was far from that. John opened it. Then he said, 'I've got the sack!'

The letter was signed by the vicar and it stated that owing to his disagreement with John about charismatic theology it had become impossible for them to work together. The vicar gave him three months' notice and he hoped that by then John would have found another post which was to his satisfaction.

We were stunned.

'I wonder why he didn't wait and tell me at the staff meeting?' John said, looking bewildered.

I stared at him. 'If he feels as strongly as that, that he cannot work with you, the next three months are going to be extremely difficult.'

A cloud hung over our Christmas, but we had planned a break immediately afterwards at Mabledon, a conference centre near Tonbridge. As we drove up the long, winding drive through the lovely grounds to the huge mansion John sighed. 'This is not going to be much of a break for me after all,' he said. 'I'm going to be very busy.'

During the few days of our stay there he wrote over thirty letters to everyone that we could think of who might be able to help him find another post.

On returning to Wunford John was summoned to report at the vicarage. After a full morning's work he arrived at the stipulated time.

The vicar apologized that he had given him three months' notice. 'It should have been six,' he explained.

He asked John if he intended to make it known.

'Of course!' John replied. 'I've nothing to be ashamed of!'

Then, before he left the vicarage, John was suspended on full pay. All items belonging to the church were to be returned immediately. We could remain in our house for six months but John would have no official duties whatsoever. He was no longer the curate, just an Anglican clergyman living in the parish. He would have no opportunity to preach there again or preside over any parochial meeting.

Once again we were shocked and angry. I flopped down on our settee and tried to adjust to the new situation.

'Surely you can't pull out of everything just like that!' I reasoned.

'Well, we can still go along to church as ordinary worshippers.'

'But that'll be very awkward for us,' I protested, 'especially when the vicar's taking the service. I wonder what everybody will think when he makes it public?'

The vicar put just a few lines about it in the parish newsletter. He wrote that he was unable to work with John any more because of differences over charismatic theology. He added that there was no question about John's good character and integrity.

After that, confusion reigned, and we were caught in the middle of it. Some churchgoers missed the notice altogether and wondered why John was sitting in the congregation. Others were at a loss to comprehend what it meant. Many, when they did, could not understand why such strong action had been taken and a number expressed their shock and disbelief. Those closest to us assured us of their love and their prayers.

As the word spread to those in the parish who did not attend church it became the cause of much more confusion. We lived in a friendly community but one day as I met Stephen from school I was aware of hostility. Outside the playground the other mothers were standing in small groups. As they chatted among themselves they stole furtive glances at me. My instinct told me that the news had reached them. Suddenly I felt very low.

When I arrived back home I said, 'I think I'll see if they

can fit me in at the hairdresser's. I need cheering up.'

The local hairdresser's was just around the corner. It was a small salon frequented mainly by clients in the immediate vicinity. I went there regularly and looked forward to the inevitable chat.

'I hear your husband's been given the sack,' the girl said as she tucked in the towel around my neck. I blushed slightly.

'Yes, that's right,' I replied. I noticed that the other women waiting had stopped reading their magazines and were listening intently.

'What did he do, then?' she asked as she shampooed my hair vigorously.

'Nothing,' I answered. 'It's just that the vicar disagreed with him over a theological matter.'

'But he must have done something!'

'No, that's all there is to it.' There was an awkward silence.

When my hair was finished I paid the bill and left quickly. The tears that were already stinging my eyes trickled down my cheeks as I rushed home to John.

'Whatever's the matter?' he asked anxiously. 'Your hair looks super.'

'They think you've done something wrong,' I choked. 'How could they?'

He gently took me in his arms. 'Can you blame them?' he said. 'The people in our own churches don't understand. How can we expect outsiders to? If you were in their shoes you would probably think exactly the same.'

'That's true, I suppose.'

'Come on,' John urged. 'Dry those tears. I expect there will be lots of rumours going around yet.'

And there were. The next one which we heard was that John must have embezzled the church funds. And yet another was that we had been holding séances in our house!

As the news of John's suspension spread further afield we began to receive telephone calls from astonished ministers asking if it was true. Many of them expressed concern and tried to encourage us. We badly needed such encouragement. Whereas before we had been at the centre of the hubbub of parish life, now we were out on a limb. We didn't seem to fit in any more and we kept wondering where we would end up.

At first we thought that we would soon find somewhere else, but it wasn't easy. In the Church of England many curates were unable to obtain livings. They were having to wait until more incumbents retired. John didn't mind remaining as a curate but if he worked with another vicar he was going to ensure that it would be one sympathetic to charismatic renewal.

The months rolled by and when John's notice expired we still had nowhere to go. We were given permission to stay on in the house, but because we now had no income John needed a job. He managed to obtain a few weeks' work with Fountain Trust and after that at the local tax office.

'What am I doing here?' he thought one day as he travelled to work on the bus. 'How much longer is this going to go on?' He stared out of the window. 'Lord, please find us somewhere soon. It's so difficult to settle down to anything!'

As he alighted and began walking to the office, a tightness seized his chest and he felt even more disheartened and downcast. He had been in a long dark tunnel and still could not see the light at the end. Now the strain was beginning to tell on his body. That night he went to the doctor, who prescribed tranquillizers.

The next day John came into the kitchen with a copy of *Church and People* magazine in his hand.

'Look at this!' he exclaimed. 'They always put reports on several Anglican churches but I've never seen one like this before.'

It was a report on St Paul's, Hainault, in Essex, where the vicar was Trevor Dearing. It told of countless people converted, healed and blessed.

'I've heard Roy mention this chap,' I recalled. 'Why don't you write to him and see if he knows of anywhere we can go?'

John did this, but not very enthusiastically, because by now he was thoroughly exhausted from the continuous fruitless effort.

One boiling hot summer's afternoon soon afterwards I

decided to take the boys to a park in Guildford. There was a
paddling pool there and I thought that they would be able to
cool off a little. They really enjoyed themselves splashing
around while I lay on the grass sunbathing.

Suddenly I heard screaming, and I saw Stephen running
towards me with blood pouring from his lips. He had slipped
and fallen, taking the full impact upon his mouth. Where his
two front teeth had been there were now two gaping holes.
His teeth had disappeared into his upper jaw.

An ambulance came for him and I followed it in the car to
the hospital. After a long wait I was told to bring him back
the next day when the dentist would be present.

Poor Stephen! When he awoke the next morning he looked
just like Donald Duck! The dentist took an instrument and,
without giving him any sedation, attempted to pull the two
teeth back down. When this was unsuccessful he told me, 'I'll
have to keep him in hospital and do it under anaesthetic.'

So Stephen was whisked off to a ward, given some pyjamas
and put to bed, and I was then told to leave. Up to then my
son had been very brave for an eight year old, but as I said
goodbye he clung to me tightly, screaming frantically.
Somehow I wrenched myself away and walked along the
lengthy corridor, his screams ringing in my ears. I drove
home in despair, wondering what was going to happen to us
next!

Not long afterwards we motored to Leeds, where John
took his brother's wedding. On the way back two of our gears
failed, and from London to Wunford we either had to use first
or fourth gear. We took the car to a garage but were told that
it was irreparable.

We needed transport, so we decided to trust the Lord for
another car. John arranged to pay £100 deposit, which we
didn't possess. On the day that it was due to be paid and the
car collected, we received a cheque through the post for
exactly that amount. It was from friends at Hailsham whom
we seldom heard from. They knew something of our circumstances, but not about the arrangements for another car.

It seemed like a miracle! It was to be six years before we

launched out into a 'faith ministry', but the Lord was already shaping us for this, teaching us in so many ways to depend entirely upon him. We began to see that our future was entirely in his hands.

Kneeling together on the blue lounge carpet, we prayed what we now believe was a dangerous prayer.

4

'Sorry, Church Full!'

Our hands were joined and our hearts united as we put our thoughts into words.

'Lord, we've tried everything we can think of and still we have nowhere to go. We know what sort of parish we should like but we want what you want. We'll do *anything* for you, we'll go *anywhere* with you.'

Before our previous moves we had always prayed, but not like this. We had put limits on the Lord. Our prayer had been—'A conservative evangelical parish, please, Lord, near a town, in the south east, south of the river Thames!' But now we were desperate and we lay ourselves unreservedly before him. We gave him permission to do anything with us and to take us anywhere.

This was a dangerous prayer to pray because undoubtedly God took us at our word. From now on John and I were to be like putty in his hands. Through many experiences he moulded us and trained us for the ministry into which he eventually led us.

At last a letter arrived that looked hopeful. It was from Peter, a rector at Buckhurst Hill, Essex.

'Trevor Dearing tells me you are looking for a post,' he wrote. 'I require a priest very soon to take charge of one of my district churches.'

When we met Peter he lay stretched out in a deck chair in his garden, almost asleep in the sun. He was very tall, dark and in his early fifties. Our conversation with him and his wife was relaxed and informal. He showed us his church, then we drove down the hill to St Elisabeth's, the district church at the far end of the parish.

'This is a dual purpose building,' he explained. 'The same room is used for Sunday worship and weekday activities.'

After that we called at the parsonage, which was spacious and seemed ideal. Peter was happy for us to go there and with a sigh of relief John accepted the invitation.

There followed a busy period of packing at Wunford and a farewell attended by people of all denominations.

After this we soon settled into our new home at Buckhurst Hill. We were very thankful to be in the centre of activities again, though St Elisabeth's was unlike all our previous churches as it was particularly known in the area for its social life. But we resolved that our main priority still would be sharing the reality of Jesus.

Stephen and Paul adapted quickly to their new surroundings and were soon exploring the neighbourhood with their friends. Opposite the parsonage was a lane leading to a large field and beyond that was the river. This was a favourite playing area. One day we heard a neighbour calling us.

'Your son Stephen's stuck up a tree over in the field. Have you got a ladder?' We had not, and there followed a frantic house to house search until we found one. We hastened to the field and I peered anxiously up at what must have been one of the largest, leafiest trees that I have ever seen.

'Stephen, where are you?' I cried out.

'Here, Mum,' came the rather shaky reply, 'right at the top!' It was obvious that the ladder would not be long enough to reach him.

'We'll have to call the fire brigade,' John shouted. 'Hold on tightly, Stephen!'

By the time that the firemen arrived there was a large crowd of spectators and they watched breathlessly as the rescue took place. Stephen rather enjoyed the attention and seemed none the worse for his ordeal.

But a few weeks later, Paul, not to be outdone, fell in the river! Apparently the water came up to his waist and Stephen dragged him out. I knew nothing about this until we sat down to tea that day and I noticed that the floor was very wet. I then saw that Paul was sitting at the table soaked to the skin and he told me of the day's adventures.

Trevor Dearing's church at Hainault was fifteen minutes' drive from where we lived, and one afternoon Peter took us to a ministers' meeting there. About forty ministers and their wives were gathered in the hall and towards the end we were intrigued to see Trevor handing out little slips of paper.

'This one's in your parish,' he explained to one clergyman. 'She was healed on Tuesday night.' He went over to a dark-haired Baptist minister. 'This chap's in your district, Gordon. He came to the Lord on Tuesday but he needs further counselling. Can you arrange that?'

After the meeting he called out above the clatter of teacups.

'This girl lives in Edmonton. Does anyone know who can follow her up?'

'Whatever happens there on Tuesday nights?' John asked Peter as he drove us home.

'That's when Trevor has his Power, Praise and Healing services,' he replied.

I turned to John and gripped his hand tightly.

'We must go to one of those, darling. When's the next Tuesday evening that you're free?'

'Let's see....' John turned over the pages of his diary. 'It'll have to be after Easter now.'

Eventually a Tuesday evening came when we were free. As we entered the council estate where St Paul's was situated we noticed that the whole area was jammed with cars and coaches, though it was some time before the service was due to begin.

The sound of bright, enthusiastic singing floated out to us as we hurried towards the building and at the door we were greeted by strong hugs and handshakes, as though we were long lost relatives.

Once inside, what a sight met our eyes! The small church

was bursting at the seams, with over five hundred people packed into it. There were people everywhere, even on the windowsills, along the aisles and in the chancel.

After the gospel message an appeal was given and we were amazed to see streams of people forming queues for the laying on of hands. As they were prayed for many seemed overcome and were gently lowered to the floor. Something real was obviously happening to them because we saw their faces change. Some were radiant and were praising the Lord aloud for their healing. Others looked peaceful and contented as they returned to their seats. We had never before encountered such a powerful atmosphere in a meeting and we found it very moving.

I felt so excited about it that I talked non-stop all the way home, and when we got to bed we found it difficult to get to sleep.

'It was just like walking into a scene from the Acts of the Apostles,' I exclaimed. 'That's what it *should* be like!'

'That's true,' said John thoughtfully. 'I can imagine a similar scene when Jesus was on earth. *He* used to preach and heal the sick like that.'

'When all those people came forward tonight,' I went on, 'it made me realize that the church in general is not reaching outsiders. But obviously *this* one is.' I opened my eyes wide. 'It must be because the news has got round that Jesus is healing people there.'

'Yes,' agreed John, 'just like in Bible times.' He shifted his head on his pillow. 'It makes you feel you want to get together all the sick folk you can and take them!'

As I dropped off to sleep I was already mentally making a list, not only of those who were sick, but of others who would benefit from being there.

In the months that followed we arranged our programme so that we were free on most Tuesday evenings. Going to the meeting at Hainault became the highlight of our week and whenever we could we took others with us.

What impressed us most was something that was to be of paramount importance to our future ministry—the power of touch in the name of Jesus.

It is interesting that properly controlled experiments have been conducted in America into healing through the laying on of hands. One of these was with three groups of mice consisting of twenty-five in each group, all with identical, induced wounds on their backs. The first group was left to heal naturally, the second was given healing through touch and the third was subjected to a lamp simulating exactly the amount of heat given off by the healer's hands. Each group's healing rate was carefully monitored. The twenty-five mice which had received healing through touch made dramatically faster recoveries than those in the other two groups.

The powerful touch of Jesus was to become one of the main characteristics of our ministry. Some people now travel many miles to receive this.

But the laying on of hands is not a magical process, neither does it necessarily produce instant results. At Hainault we saw people cured of a great variety of diseases. Some were healed straight away, some during the following days, others over a period of weeks or months. Yet others appeared to receive no obvious physical healing but they still kept coming for ministry because of the benefits which they received spiritually, emotionally or mentally.

It was at St Paul's that we first came to understand clearly that sickness was an evil to be fought against like sin—that God allows it but does not send it. We saw that Jesus died on the cross not only to save us from our sin but to heal us from our sicknesses, just as Isaiah prophesied:

'He was wounded for our transgressions, he was bruised for our iniquities; upon him was the chastisement that made us whole, and with his stripes we are healed' (Isaiah 53:5).

We also began to grasp that Jesus has given authority to *all* his disciples to preach the gospel and heal the sick. Gradually it dawned on us that we had only been obeying the first half of this command.

When John was chaplain at Worthing Hospital he had prayed for many patients but it had never occurred to him to minister the laying on of hands for healing and when praying for the sick he would often add the phrase, 'if it be your will'. But now we decided to pray more positively and also to minister if the opportunity presented itself.

As we left St Paul's one evening we noticed a sign outside: 'Sorry, church full!'

'What a pity that so many people have to converge on one particular church!' I remarked to John. 'If more churches held meetings like that it wouldn't be necessary.'

On another Tuesday at Hainault Trevor unexpectedly announced: 'There's a clergyman here whom I believe the Lord is calling into a healing ministry. If John Huggett will come forward we should like to commission him.'

My husband pushed his way through to the front and several ministers gathered around him. A hush fell as they laid their hands upon him and Trevor led the congregation in praying that the Lord would equip him, especially with gifts of healing.

Immediately after this John found himself faced with queues of people and tentatively began laying hands upon them. He continued to minister alongside Trevor and others every Tuesday.

The news soon spread that people were being blessed through John's ministry at Hainault and various needy folk from outside our parish came knocking at our door for help.

About this time we started fellowship meetings in our home for those interested in renewal. Barbara, a Christian lady living in Woodford Green, came along with her husband. Barbara has since written down what happened to her at one of these meetings:

> After singing some choruses we joined hands in a circle to pray. Being very English and reserved, I was rather surprised at this practice. However, as John came from playing the piano to join the circle I held his hand. We prayed for a while and I felt my head nod as if I was dozing and thought I had better concentrate harder!
>
> I should point out that since I was nine I had no hearing in one ear due to the eardrum being badly damaged by an abscess. I managed fairly well with one good ear but it was an embarrass-

ment at formal dinners when I had to explain to the person on my right side that I could not hear him without turning my head. I had never heard my children in the night as I slept with my deaf ear uppermost.

Three days after the meeting every sound seemed so loud. I tested this by covering up my good ear. I was amazed and excited. I could hear bird song extremely clearly—it was like the difference between radio and hi fi. However, sleep was difficult as I was unused to hearing our neighbour's dog barking!

I praise the Lord for the healing through John. Our Lord knew what I needed without my asking him.

In recent years we have been back to take healing meetings at Woodford and have found that Barbara's healing has been permanent.

She writes of something else which happened shortly after that meeting in our parsonage.

'My younger son took his friend with asthma to a meeting where John laid hands on him. He was cured. He was able to take part in games again and had no need of what he called his puffer.'

A steady flow of people were being blessed. One of my friends suffered from claustrophobia. In meetings she sat at the end of a row so that she could run out quickly if panic seized her, but after prayer over a period of time her problem disappeared. A lady who had attended church for forty years knelt in her home and received Christ into her life. A very old man who we thought that the Lord would heal by taking him to be with himself recovered remarkably after ministry and lived on for several years! Two young mothers who came for their children to be baptized found Jesus for themselves and were confirmed.

Just before Christmas our butcher called at the parsonage with some meat for us. He looked worried.

'There's a shortage of turkeys,' he said glumly. 'I can't get enough of them. I've been trying in London but now I'm concerned that I shan't be able to supply my customers' orders in time for Christmas. I've never let them down before.'

Colin belonged to St Elisabeth's and we told him that we would pray about his turkeys. As soon as he had gone I said to John, 'Let's become two in agreement for him.' We joined hands and claimed Jesus' promise that if two of us agreed about anything on earth it would be done in heaven.

'We agree that you will provide turkeys in abundance for Colin in time for Christmas, Lord, and we thank you that it's done.'

At the midnight communion service on Christmas Eve we could see by Colin's face that all was well.

'Yes,' he said, beaming, 'plenty of turkeys, just in time!'

Vera was in her early twenties but she looked much younger. She was small and slim with long dark hair. One Sunday morning she appeared at the Family Service asking for help.

'I've heard you do healing here,' she said. 'I've come because I suffer from epilepsy.' John and I learnt that she lived in the same road as we did, and we arranged to visit her during the week.

When we arrived we discovered that Vera and her husband had been very much involved with the occult. She regularly talked with apparitions and her husband practised automatic writing. We had a long discussion with them both, explaining what it would mean if Vera came to Jesus for help.

'He can set you free,' John said gently, 'but you will have to renounce these practices and not dabble in them again.'

We took Vera to Hainault, where several evil spirits were cast out of her, and she joined our Wednesday morning ladies' group at the parsonage. But as soon as God's power was released among us each week she collapsed on the floor in what we discerned was a demonic fit. Several times we stopped the meetings and spent a long time ministering to her. However, after a few weeks I said to John, 'I think the devil is trying to get our eyes off Jesus. Vera's getting all the attention in these meetings. Have you noticed how long it's taking to minister to her?'

'Yes,' he agreed. 'It's not fair on the others. I think next time we'll just bind the spirit and let her lie there until afterwards.' And we did!

We seemed to attract people in need. We met Julie when we were on holiday, at a Christian hotel in Devon. She approached us hesitantly.

'Will you pray for me?' she enquired. 'I need God's help as my husband goes into violent and uncontrollable rages.'

I laid my hands on her head and began to pray. As I did I was hit by blackness and I recognized that Satan was in this situation. Immediately I took authority over him in the name of Jesus. We met up with Julie and her husband several times after our holiday and were able to take them to receive more help at Hainault.

'Our life's becoming too unbalanced,' I said to John one afternoon. I had just closed the parsonage door behind yet another person who had come for prayer. 'I feel I need to do something entirely different or else I shall go mad! It's encouraging to help people but not to the exclusion of every-thing else. I think I'll attempt to pass an audition for "The Thistles".'

'The Thistles', an operatic society, was planning to put on the musical *A Wedding in Paris*, and I was accepted to sing in the chorus. I made some new friends and thoroughly enjoyed myself. After all the performances were over I felt stimulated and refreshed and back on top form again.

One of our pleasant duties was to accompany the Senior Citizens on their annual outing to the seaside. After a lovely day at Southend-on-Sea we were returning home on the coach when there was a loud explosion. The whole of the front windscreen had shattered, showering glass everywhere. I was wearing open sandals, and a splinter of glass embedded itself into my heel.

When we arrived back that evening we had a confirmation class in our house. Everyone tried to remove the glass with tweezers but it would not budge! So off to the hospital I went. There the nurse asked me to lie on my stomach and then she rammed a needle into the sole of my foot. It was very painful and I yelled loudly. Extricating the glass after that proved to be no problem!

Later my thoughts turned to Jesus. He had undergone not a needle in one foot but long nails driven through both feet and both hands as well.

'Thank you, Jesus,' I breathed, 'for the physical pain which you endured for me.'

Unpredictability was the hallmark of our life. We began to wonder what each knock on our door would bring. One day, when we were interrupted by urgent banging, we opened the door to a lady who lived not far from us.

'There's someone lying out there in the middle of the road,' she said, 'I believe you know her.'

'Whatever's happened this time?' John muttered to me as we followed our neighbour down the parsonage steps.

'I wonder who it is?' I whispered back.

When we reached the spot we saw a familiar figure sprawled out before us.

It was Vera.

5

Stumped and Thumped

Almost as if she sensed that we were there she opened her eyes and stared up at us.

'I must have had a fit,' she murmured weakly.

We helped Vera to her feet and sat with her on a garden wall nearby. Then her husband arrived and we thankfully left her with him.

'I'm stumped!' I said flatly as we walked back to the parsonage. 'Why does she still have these fits when she's received so much ministry? I can't understand it.'

'Neither can I.' John look puzzled. 'She seems worse than ever.'

We soon learned the reason. Vera had not attempted to curtail her occult activities, in spite of our advice to her that she should. No wonder that we could not make any progress! As fast as the spirits were leaving her she was as good as inviting them back. We had wasted much precious time with her but had learned a valuable lesson: it is no use endeavouring to help people unless they are willing to help themselves.

Not far from Vera lived Clare, a lady in her early fifties. John visited her in hospital after she had had an operation for cancer.

'I used to go to church but I'm afraid I've let it slip,' she confessed.

'Well,' John said gently, 'when you are well again you

51

must come to St Elisabeth's.'

A few weeks later she did and was soon asking if she could be confirmed. She then joined the confirmation group at the parsonage and we came to know her very well. We prayed for healing from the cancer but after several months signs of the disease returned and it soon began to take its toll upon her body. Yet Clare seemed to blossom and in spirit she became noticeably stronger. This was very evident one Sunday evening in church when she gave her testimony.

'I want you all to know that these last few months have been the happiest of my life,' she said. 'I've found Jesus.'

Shortly after this Clare deteriorated even more and was confined to her bedroom. When we visited her she was sitting beside the window. She was little more than a skeleton and her breathing was very laboured.

'It won't be long now, will it?' she whispered. I looked helplessly at John. Words seemed superfluous somehow. We held her hand a while, then left. Later when we saw her she was saying the twenty-third psalm, and a few hours after that she died.

'What a triumph!' I said to John. 'She rose above that disease. It didn't touch her, not in her spirit.' We couldn't help thinking of the words of Romans 8:37–39: 'We are more than conquerors through him who loved us. For I am sure that neither death, nor life...nor anything else in all creation, will be able to separate us from the love of God in Christ Jesus our Lord.'

A few months later, in a brief encounter with a previous curate, we were introduced to Victorious Ministry for Christ. Lionel had just been on one of their prayer counselling schools and was bubbling over with enthusiasm about what he had learned and experienced there.

After listening to him I said, 'We need to go on something like that. We want to make progress.'

'I'll nominate you then,' promised Lionel.

That spring we arrived at a convent near Bedford for a prayer counselling school and for four days we worked intensely from morning till night with about twenty other ministers and their wives.

The first part of each day was filled with lectures. We were reminded that we can all be bound to habits, fears, circumstances and negative attitudes. We can also be bound to people in unhelpful ways, especially our parents and those closest to us. But the Lord can set us free from these invisible chains. He has given us his word, the sword of the Spirit, to cut right through them. Sometimes the bonds are too strong for us to break through by our own prayers and we need experienced Christians to do it for us in Jesus' name.

Negative attitudes, such as guilt and resentment, can damage us inwardly and affect our health. But the Lord will replace them with positive ones, like love and forgiveness, as we cooperate with him.

What interested me most was the healing of the memories, for I knew that I needed this. The leaders reminded us that we act and react according to our backgrounds, that we are all products of our yesterdays. Memories of traumatic events, together with hurts and wounds, are stored in our subconscious minds and lie buried there. Because Jesus is the same yesterday, today and for ever he can go back in time and heal these things, dealing with them at their very root. We can go back with him in our imagination as he gently soothes away the pains of the past.

This is rather like peeling an onion. He begins with the outer layer and removes a layer at a time, as we are ready, gradually working deeper. This doesn't mean that incidents are forgotten, but that we are released from the painful effects which they have had upon us, so discovering a new freedom.

Prayer counselling, we were told, is absolutely confidential. It doesn't consist of giving advice but of listening and praying. The Christian receiving this talks about himself, sometimes for hours. The counsellors listen with one ear open to the Lord, who points out through natural and supernatural revelations how he wants them to pray. Each matter is then prayed about in detail, as led by the Holy Spirit, with laying on of hands. Usually the negative things are dealt with first, followed by ministry for healing and the fullness of the Holy

Spirit. Finally the person is encouraged to put on the whole armour of God.

After several lectures the Anglican clergyman leading the school announced: 'We're shortly going to minister to you individually, and we've asked the Lord in which order to take you. When each of you has been prayer counselled you will assist with prayer counselling others. Now the first one of all will be Christine Huggett.'

'I *would* be first!' I thought, a trifle apprehensively.

When my appointment time arrived I entered the small room where three counsellors were waiting for me, two men and a woman. I could feel the love of Jesus in that room as they listened to my story and prayed about my memories. At the end I felt peaceful and thoroughly loved. It was a wonderful experience.

I went searching for John and told him what had happened. To my amazement I discovered that my session had lasted for four and a quarter hours! During that period my husband had been prayer counselled and had ministered to someone else. We had both talked so much that it was a relief to relax for our evening meal. But we hardly had time to digest this before we were back to work again.

On the last day of the conference the whole morning was devoted to an open time of praise and testimony. We gathered in a large circle and two chairs were placed in the centre. Each person in turn sat on one of them and was prayed for. Married couples sat together. The Lord spoke through prophecy to most people and we noticed how encouraging the words were. However, when our turn came, the message included some rather strange words: 'I shall not take from you anything other than that which I desire.'

I thought back to my forebodings about Paul and felt rather anxious.

'I feel worried now,' I whispered to John. 'I hope those words don't mean that somebody's going to die.'

We had left the children at the rectory during the conference and driving back to Buckhurst Hill to collect them we enthusiastically discussed the happenings of the last four days.

'What struck me most was the loving way in which they ministered to us,' I said when we were out on the open road.

'Yes. I was impressed by their policy of no condemnation,' John recalled. 'It's true. God doesn't condemn Christians, for Paul wrote that there's no condemnation to those in Christ Jesus. Yet we often condemn one another! Before we start our prayer counselling in the parish I'd like to resolve never to condemn anyone, regardless of what a person confesses. Obviously we can't condone sin, but it's the Lord's business to judge people, not ours.'

I nodded in agreement.

'So much of what we've learned is going to be invaluable in the parish,' John added as we slowed down at a roundabout. We'll probably have to adapt it, though. Every situation is different.'

'I can't wait to put it all into practice!' I smiled.

We picked up speed and headed confidently for home.

The first person to come to us for prayer counselling at the parsonage was a young lady called Jill. When she had sat down on the settee John said, 'Now, tell us in your own words what most bothers you.'

There was dead silence and for the next two hours we could hardly get a word out of her.

The Lord has a marvellous sense of humour. All that we had learned about listening patiently while the person shared at length went straight out of the window. For Jill's problem was that she simply could not communicate! We had to rely totally upon the Lord to show us her situation. We spent six hours with her that night and a further four hours on a subsequent evening before her prayer counselling was complete.

We learned from this experience not to have such long sessions but to invite people back several times if necessary. We later learned that some people may need further ministry in the future if they experienced more traumas or the Lord uncovered deeper problems.

Martha was very different from Jill. She was in her sixties and had no difficulty in sharing about what particularly

worried her—a recurring nightmare which had haunted her
for years. She had also repressed her emotions and for many
years had shed no tears.

Martha was thirsty for the release of the Holy Spirit, so
besides praying for inner healing we asked the Lord to fill her
to overflowing. As we did this she visibly relaxed and
appeared to pass out completely!

While in this condition Martha started crying, with deep,
heart-rending sobs. It appeared that all the tears of the years
were pouring out of her, and along with them she spoke in
tongues. After a while she opened her eyes and sat up.

'You've been baptized in the Holy Spirit,' I told her, 'and
you spoke in tongues.'

'Oh, and I missed it!' she exclaimed, reaching for a tissue
and drying her eyes. 'I missed it!' But she was radiant.

'There must be a reason why it happened to you like that,'
my husband assured her. 'It's as though the Lord put you
under a divine anaesthetic. Perhaps it would have been too
painful for you otherwise. You've certainly had a wonderful
release.'

This was confirmed in the weeks that followed. Martha's
nightmare had disappeared for good and she was a different
person.

We began to find that people who were physically sick
frequently needed inner healing as well. As we were ministering this the Lord sometimes gave me pictures of incidents
in the person's past. Often this would trigger off a memory
which needed healing. On some occasions the picture was
not self-explanatory but John would be given the interpretation. It was an awesome and faith-building experience to
see the Lord release people at a deep level before our eyes.

Soon it was holiday time again. Everyone in our family
was excited about going to Jersey, as it was our first trip there
and our first journey in a plane. But when we boarded and
the doors were closed I was terrified! During the flight I
clung tightly to John. The boys couldn't understand my fear.
They thought it was great to be up so high and Stephen was
busy showing Graham, his teddy bear, the view from the

window.

We loved the island, particularly the little bays, which were surprisingly quiet and clean, even during the peak holiday period. There were several castles for the boys to explore and plenty to occupy us all. But towards the end of our week I began to dread returning home. It was not just the flight that worried me. John had recently been overworking in the parish and the only time that I seemed to see him was when we ministered together to someone in the parsonage. I wished that I could see more of him because I had so appreciated his company that holiday week.

We prayed about the flight back and much to my delight I really enjoyed it. On several occasions since, the Lord has promised me, 'I will take away your fear of flying.'

John and I looked forward eagerly to the monthly meetings of the Buckhurst Hill Charismatic Fellowship, which were held in our home. Christians from different churches attended these. Frank, the local Pentecostal pastor, came regularly with his wife. They were used to exercising the gifts of the Spirit and took a lead in doing this. This was a great encouragement to us and John began to step out in the gift of prophecy.

'It's just like opening a packet of tissues,' he said jokingly. 'I receive a few words in my mind and as I speak them out I'm given a few more, and so on, until it suddenly stops. Sometimes I'm given a picture which I know I'm to describe. As I share it other pictures or words follow.'

One evening one of John's prophecies began with the words, 'Let not the grass grow under your feet.' The speaker on this occasion was an Anglican clergyman and afterwards he asked us, 'Are you thinking of moving? I believe that word from the Lord was for you personally.'

'Well,' John answered, 'I have been looking for a living for some time now, but as you know, you have to be offered one—you can't just apply.'

'Isn't it wonderful how the Lord speaks so directly in these meetings!' I enthused as we talked about it later that night. '*I* want to share the gifts in them, too, but somehow I just don't know how to get started.'

I began to pray that the Lord would show me how—and he did, rather unexpectedly! One particular evening about fifteen of us were gathered in our lounge. Sitting in a relaxed circle, we began our meeting by worshipping the Lord. After that we had an open time when individuals who felt led could pray or start up a chorus. The atmosphere was very informal. My eyes were closed and I was entering into the spirit of the meeting.

Suddenly I felt as if an invisible person had given me a thump in the stomach. I opened my eyes wide in alarm. Thump! There it was again! Then it was coming at regular intervals. And something else was happening, too: my tongue was moving uncontrollably inside my mouth. It was as though I should be speaking, but I didn't know what to say.

I glanced around nervously. 'I think I've got to say something,' I said in a small voice.

I thought that someone must surely help me. But all eyes remained tightly closed. 'Well, here goes then,' I said to myself. 'I'll have to speak it out. At least I'm among friends if I make a fool of myself!'

Hesitantly I gave my first gift of tongues to the meeting. There was a short silence and then Frank gave a beautiful interpretation. I heaved a sigh of relief because the Bible says that if the gift of tongues is used in public and not interpreted you should pray for the interpretation yourself. I didn't have the courage to give a tongue and interpret it too!

From then on 'the thumps', as we affectionately call it, became a sign that God wanted me to speak out a tongue during a meeting, which I did at appropriate times. I would give the tongue until the thumps ceased. Then I knew that it was right to stop speaking.

I was beginning to get used to such manifestations of the Lord's power upon me. One day my hands began to vibrate and burn again and he reminded me that he was going to use them much more. He seemed to be in no hurry, though!

It was a cold day in February when I opened a letter offering John two parishes in the north. He was just off out. I could hear him starting the car outside and I rushed to the front door to call him back.

The letter looked very promising. The invitation was to be vicar of two parishes—Merston Mill and Wilfirth, small Yorkshire villages just outside Huddersfield. Merston Mill, the larger parish, said that they had been experiencing renewal and asked for a man with 'Holy Spirit ministry'. Wilfirth, which had a population of just two or three hundred, would be sharing a vicar for the first time.

After reading through the lengthy letter John looked up. 'It seems just right for me,' he said. 'What do you think, darling?'

'I think you ought to have a look at it. I've a feeling we'll be going there.'

A few weeks later John travelled the two hundred miles up the motorway to meet the churchwardens and look over the parishes. As he neared Huddersfield he had a pleasant surprise.'

'I imagined it would be smokier and grimier than this,' he thought. 'The houses are a drab grey but the industry hasn't spoilt the countryside.'

During his two days in Huddersfield he was shown both parishes and he warmed very much to the prospect of moving there.

'I feel generally happy about what I've seen,' he thought on the way home. 'But it would be very different from any of our parishes in the south. I must try to remember all the relevant points to describe to Chris. She'll be longing to see it, especially the vicarage.'

After listening to John's full description of the two parishes, I felt sure that we were to go there. The set-up seemed tailor-made for us and the vast Victorian vicarage sounded marvellous.

'It would take a lot of looking after, though,' I remarked, 'and so would the garden. But it would be lovely to move there. Did you say there's no church hall?'

'That's right, not at Merston Mill where we'd be living. They use the vicarage.'

I tried to picture the scene but it was difficult. However, I didn't have long to wait before seeing it, for John wrote and accepted the offer.

By now Trevor Dearing had left Hainault to devote himself full time to evangelism and healing. The ministers' meeting continued in his home at Ilford. We went along to it for the last time shortly before we were due to move north.

Several ministers prayed aloud for our new work and then hands were laid on us to commission us. There were two beautiful prophecies which forecast that many people would be blessed through our future ministry. As these were spoken a ripple of praise broke out among those present.

But then Trevor began to speak in a very solemn tone and a deathly silence descended. His hands were on my head at the time and as he prophesied I felt my heart sinking lower and lower.

6

'Among Those Dark Satanic Mills'

'Soon after you get there you will be under strong attack. This will come from behind you.' Trevor's voice maintained the note of solemnity as he continued. 'It will strike like an axe hacking at you with relentless persistence.'

My heart was in my boots' by now and I felt John's hand groping for mine. He gripped it firmly. The prophecy went on for ages, all in the same vein, and only the last few words provided a glimmer of hope: 'Eventually, with much love and patience, you will triumph over it.'

Feeling somewhat deflated we drove home.

'What did it all mean?' I said with dismay.

'I don't know,' John sighed. 'It wasn't very uplifting, not like prophecies usually are. But I'm sure it was from the Lord.'

'Yes, so am I. But it's left me feeling that I don't want to move to the north now. It's a big enough wrench leaving all our friends in the south, without going into a situation where we know we're going to have trouble.'

'I feel the same,' he said sympathetically, 'but it's all been fixed now and I feel sure it's in the Lord's plan for us to go.'

After lunch we remained at the table to pray about the whole matter. Almost immediately John had some words: 'I'm sending you to a strange people.'

Then, as we waited on the Lord, some pictures came into John's mind and he began to describe them.

61

'We're in a dark room,' he said, 'and we're fumbling to find the door.' There was a short pause. 'Now we're going through it, and we're in another dark room. There's a series of them. We're wandering through them, one after another, in almost total blackness. Now we've come into a bright room. I can see a large treasure chest in the centre. It's wide open and filled to overflowing with glittering jewels!'

I opened my eyes and stared at the empty plates in front of me.

'Our immediate future doesn't look too rosy,' I said grimly.

'That's an understatement,' commented my husband dryly. He jumped up and gave me a big kiss. 'Come on, let's do this washing up. Whatever happens the Lord is with us and we have each other.'

The following days we worked towards our move. People still kept coming for ministry, though, so we counselled them among the packing cases.

'I do hope we stay up north a while,' I thought. 'As John is going to be a vicar this time perhaps we can be more settled.'

We had a very pleasant farewell gathering, and then moving day at last dawned. It was early June. There was a drought and the removal men perspired under the heat. It turned out to be one of the hottest days of the year. We were staying overnight with one of the churchwardens and his family, having arranged to meet the lorry at Merston Mill vicarage the following day. By the time that we arrived at our hosts' house we were hot and sticky and extremely tired. In spite of this, I hardly slept a wink that night.

'Here we are in a strange place among strange people,' I thought, 'and all our belongings are in a lorry somewhere!'

But in the light of morning things looked different. We drove to the vicarage and began to arrange the furniture in our new home.

There were so many rooms that we didn't know where to start. The boys made straight for the cellar, which was cool and a little bit eerie. My first priority was the kitchen. It was bright and pleasant, with plenty of working surfaces. One window overlooked the garden by the front entrance and through the other window we could see cows grazing in the fields and hills in the distance.

John was eager to unpack his books in the study. From the kitchen this was a fair walk, through the long hall with the imposing staircase on the right, and past the utility room, cloakroom, dining room and huge lounge on the left. Above were five spacious bedrooms.

The house was surrounded by extensive lawns, dominated on one side by the largest horse chestnut tree in the district. In a secluded spot there was also a small vegetable garden. We were separated from the church and churchyard by a rough piece of ground which churchgoers used as a car park.

John's institution service was an inspiring occasion and it was lovely to have our parents there. The bishop reminded everyone in the full church that their new vicar was God's gift to them.

As we chatted to people afterwards we found it difficult in some cases to understand what they were saying. Some words were missed out and others had a different meaning from the one we were used to. When we heard someone say that they had landed at six we thought that they must have been in a plane, but it was their way of saying that they had arrived home. Someone else left us with, 'We woon't see ya while Soondi.' Another asked us about the vicarage: 'Do ya like?'

Most difficult of all to interpret was a question from a dark-haired man who said he 'worked in fact'ri'.

'Is moorbah?' he enquired.

'I beg your pardon?' John's educated southern accent sounded somehow out of place.

'Is moorbah?'

We finally deciphered the man's Yorkshire code. 'Is mower back?' The mower at the vicarage had been taken away for repair.

We had moved at half-term, and Stephen, who was now nearly eleven, only had a few weeks left of primary school education. I took him and his eight year old brother to their school, just a short walk along the road.

Having settled them in, I wandered around Merston village to see what shops there were. I bought some hot bread from the bakery and then, as I left, I was approached by a stranger who obviously recognized me.

'Hello loov, 'ow are ya? 'Ow's vicar?'

I wondered for a moment why she should be asking me how a vicar was. Then I remembered that the vicar was my husband!

The following Sunday morning John took his first service at Merston Mill. The congregation consisted mainly of youngish families. Some came from a large estate. Most of the men who lived there worked in the local factory.

After the service John had no time to speak to anybody. He had to dash off, still in his robes, to take the service at Wilfirth. The village there was a completely separate community out in the country, retaining much of its original Victorian atmosphere.

'I expect I'll get used to going from one church to the other every week,' thought John as he drove up into the hills.

After the Wilfirth service we had a late lunch, then decided to explore the countryside opposite the vicarage. We started to follow the footpath. Past the shabby old mill, over a quaint little bridge, we strolled towards the village of Heyne. But we heard the sound of running water and discovered nearby a waterfall and a rippling brook. We relaxed on the grass beside them and began sharing with each other our first impressions of the churches. Eventually I said, 'I keep wondering where the axe is going to strike from.'

John looked at me. 'Do you think "from behind" means from where we've just come,' he said slowly, 'or could it mean from people who are apparently behind us in what we're doing?'

'I don't know,' I answered, idly plucking a blade of grass. 'I find I'm viewing everyone and everything a little suspiciously.'

John lay back and shielded his eyes from the sun.

'It could simply mean it's going to come from where we least expect it,' he suggested.

As we later scrambled to our feet the picture of the over-flowing treasure chest came to mind.

'At least there will be triumph in the end,' I said as John took my hand and we continued our walk.

Further confirmation of what the Lord had promised was to come from a different source. We were in Hull for a few days, staying with John's brother Christopher and his wife. They badly needed some guidance about their future and one night they asked us to pray with them.

We all waited in silence a while in case the Lord wished to speak through the gifts of the Spirit. He did, but not to them as we had expected. Christopher, knowing nothing of our previous prophecies, spoke the words very softly: 'The Lord is saying, John and Chris, that an earthquake is going to erupt and you are going to be in the centre of it.'

'Oh dear!' I thought. 'Whatever's going to happen seems inevitable.'

When we arrived back home and the autumn sessions began John shared the prophecy with some of the church leaders who met regularly in the vicarage. He felt that they should be told what the Lord was saying and we needed them to pray about it.

Meetings like these in our home meant more housework for me, especially when the ground outside was wet and muddy. I seemed to be for ever cleaning. I would start at one end of the house and by the time that I had finished I had to begin all over again.

One day I was scrubbing the bath when I felt a thump.

'It can't be!' I thought incredulously. But it came again, more strongly this time—and then again.

'Help!' I thought. 'What shall I do?—I know, I'll ignore it. Perhaps it'll go away.' But it still gently persisted.

John was downstairs working in the study, so I ran to the landing and called him.

'Darling!' I shouted. 'I've got the thumps!'

He came out of the study and looked up at me.

'It must mean the Lord wants to speak to us then,' he said, smiling as he watched my active stomach.

65

'This is ridiculous!' I explained. 'He can't! We're not in a meeting!'

'Of course he can!' responded my husband as he made his way up the stairs to join me. 'Why should we limit him? You give the tongue and let's see if he gives me an interpretation.'

So just where we were standing we closed our eyes and I spoke out. John's interpretation followed swiftly: 'I am always with you wherever you are,' says the Lord. 'Search the Scriptures and you will find my gifts manifested in many different situations. I desire to converse with my children and I do this in various ways. This is one way in particular that I've chosen to speak with you. Do not be surprised at anything. I am the Lord God Almighty. My power will come upon you in unexpected places. I love you and have a plan for you.'

I suddenly became aware that I was still holding the scouring powder in one hand and a cleaning rag in the other and I burst out laughing. It had all happened so naturally, and I just went back to cleaning the bathroom.

After this the thumps became a regular part of our everyday life. Whenever the Lord wants to speak to us using this method he interrupts what we are doing by thumping me! It's like having an extra person living with us. It happens in all sorts of places, particularly at times when our thoughts are on something else.

Even when we are out shopping together he occasionally speaks to us in this way. One day in a small Merston supermarket this was overheard and later a man remarked to one of our church members, 'The vicar's wife's a foreigner, isn't she?'

One morning soon after this John returned from a ministers' meeting looking rather crestfallen.

'What a waste of time!' He was mildly annoyed as he entered the kitchen and put down his briefcase. 'They were discussing matters that we finished with down south ten years ago,' he said. 'I knew that they were behind in the northern villages but didn't realize by how much.'

I offered him a cup of coffee.

'I think we're both missing the depth of fellowship we've been used to,' I responded. 'I've heard there's a good interdenominational charismatic meeting in Halifax. Perhaps we can go.' I pulled up a chair to the table and sat opposite him.

'Yes,' he agreed. 'But I was hoping for more deep fellowship in our own churches. We were led to believe that Merston Mill had been in renewal for several years, but the signs so far are very disappointing.'

'I feel rather restless at the moment,' I said candidly. 'I shall not be really happy until you start the laying on of hands here.'

'Well, I'll have to bring in things like that gradually. They're not used to it in any degree. There should be an opportunity soon, though. I've been asked to talk about healing at the parish weekend in November and you know I don't like speaking about it without actually ministering.'

'Crumbs!' I exclaimed. 'What will they think when the power's released visibly and people start falling down?'

John was thoughtful as he drank the remainder of his coffee. 'I don't know. We've been so used to it, but it may take them a while to adjust. Don't worry, darling, the Lord will guide us step by step.'

John worked hard at preparing for the parish weekend. When it arrived, forty church members gathered in the lounge for the opening session on the Friday evening. There was a relaxed atmosphere as I closed the autumn coloured curtains across the massive bay windows and then sat down on the pouffe by the piano.

During the first session we concentrated on why it is necessary to have Christian healing alongside that provided by the medical world and others. John read the relevant scriptures and shared how we live in a sick world and all have to die sometime.

'One day there'll be no more suffering,' he said. 'But until that day comes we have a task to fulfil. On several occasions Jesus commanded his followers to heal the sick and minister to those in need. For one of the things that God desires is for everyone to be whole: in body, mind and spirit.'

On the Saturday morning a film about St Paul's, Hainault, which had been on television, was shown in church. To enable people to attend this and the other sessions, children's meetings were held elsewhere at the same time. But we all joined together in the vicarage for a fellowship lunch. We used both the dining room and the study to eat in, so that people could sit down properly and enjoy the sumptuous spread provided for them.

In the next session we tackled the question of why people are sometimes not healed, even after regular ministry. We concluded that there are many reasons and many mysteries. Sometimes God may require a specific response from the person in need before healing will take place.

The last session dealt with practical helps to wholeness. We concluded that, although some people are given gifts or ministries of healing, the Lord may call upon any one of us at any time to minister it. John encouraged us to make use of every good means available to facilitate this.

Much to our delight one of the main decisions reached at the weekend was that healing should be a normal part of the church's work. The best time to minister this regularly at Merston Mill seemed to be at the weekly Family Service. So that is what we decided to do, beginning the next day.

At the last meeting on the Saturday there was a high note of expectancy in our lounge as we met together and took communion. It was natural to put into practice what we had been talking about all day, so John offered the laying on of hands to anyone who would like it. As he touched people in Jesus' name some sank to the floor. The power of the Lord flowed freely among us throughout the meeting.

John and I went to bed feeling exhausted, but rejoicing.

Next morning at the Family Service John encouraged the church to go forward together.

'We can be like marbles,' he said, 'knocking against one another and bouncing back again. Alternatively we can be like grapes, allowing the Lord to squash us together so that he can bring out of us his new wine. If you are willing for this and want to go on with Jesus, will you come to the front and make your response to him?'

Straight away an elderly lady walked briskly to the front. There was a few moments' pause and then, one by one, nearly the whole church joined her. My husband ministered to those with particular needs; then we ended the service in a circle with hands joined.

As John and I emerged into the dull November morning we felt fully satisfied with all that had happened that weekend.

The following Sunday we were due to go to lunch with Evelyn and Joe at their home on the estate. Joe was the dark-haired man who had asked, 'Is moorbah?' Later he had been baptized in the Holy Spirit at the vicarage. Evelyn was small and cheerful and soft-spoken. She had been the first to fall under the power at the parish weekend. They were about our age and we got on very well with them.

As we drove there John said, 'I mislaid my notes at the Wilfirth service this morning. I had to preach the sermon without them. Then afterwards, when it was too late, I discovered them on the lectern, only a few yards away! Anyway, the Lord gave me the words.'

When we arrived at Evelyn and Joe's and were seated at the dining table Evelyn brought in our plates. They were completely covered with Yorkshire pudding! We stared.

'Oh, 'tis Yorkshire wey,' she giggled. 'We eat pudding first and have meat and vegetables after.'. The pudding was delicious, almost a meal in itself.

After lunch she poured out the tea and passed a jug of milk for us to add our own.

'I'm getting used to this, too,' I remarked, '—putting the milk in last instead of first.'

'I'm sending you to a strange people,' whispered John.

I smiled. But I had no inkling then of the strange behaviour that *I* was to adopt at times, starting in the near future!

'You are steyin' tea as well, aren't ya?' asked Joe.

'Yes, please!' we replied in unison.

7

Manifestations of Power

'What are you watching?' asked John as he entered the lounge.

'It's the Christmas show jumping from Olympia,' I told him. 'It's good. The children were fast asleep so I switched on the TV to see what was on.'

My husband sat down and watched while one or two more leading riders tried for clear rounds in the arena. But he was soon shifting about restlessly.

'What's the matter?' I enquired. 'How did the church council meeting go?'

'Not too badly.' His reply was cautious. 'We covered quite a lot of ground on church maintenance.'

'How about the parish weekend and the laying on of hands at the meetings?'

He looked at me and I noticed how tired he was.

'There's no doubt the weekend made a real impact and the ministry's still going ahead, but....' John's voice trailed off.

'But what?' I urged him.

'But the Lord coming down in power like he did has certainly disturbed some people. They seem particularly hung up on the falling down, and they cannot seem to see past that to what's been happening in people's lives.'

'Just as I feared!' I said. 'Didn't you get a chance to explain that it's a release of power and has happened all through church history, especially during revivals?'

'No, I didn't. I could have shown them incidents in the Bible, like when the soldiers fell backwards in the garden of Gethsemane, but I didn't want to make an issue out of it. It's an outward sign that many Christians accept readily enough. After all, we are dealing with a supernatural God.' He grinned. 'What would some of these people do if the building began to shake? We've a long way to go yet!'

There was a pause while we watched the final round of the show jumping.

'I really enjoyed that,' I said afterwards. 'I didn't realize until tonight that I liked horses so much.'

John looked at me rather vaguely, his mind still occupied.

'The devil hates the laying on of hands,' he continued. 'It's such a powerful ministry. We always have a comeback when something special happens.'

'Well,' I said cheerfully, 'it won't be special if we're going to make it part of the normal work of the church.'

Suddenly I jumped up. 'Gosh!' I exclaimed. 'I've just remembered. There are some mince pies in the oven.'

After Christmas there was a nip in the air. The hills around Merston were capped with snow and there were patches of black ice on the roads.

On Sundays the churches were usually warm, but sometimes the boiler at Merston Mill church went out and John might have to check it at one o'clock in the morning. At such times he had been known to pray it into action!

Some of the church leaders were now sharing in the laying on of hands at the Family Service each week. There were always a few folk who availed themselves of this ministry. Some people travelled especially to receive it. Sometimes I would have a tongue at this freer time in the service and John might give the interpretation. Occasionally he would prophesy. One morning the Lord said:

'My train is coming this way and I am calling you all to get on board. I am the ticket collector who admits you. The Holy Spirit is the driver who leads you on and my Father is the guard who takes care of all on board. Do not get left behind. I want to take you on to your next destination. I have so much more for you.'

As I sat and listened I wondered how many in the church were even *on* the train. And those who were, did they really want to be led by the driver? When we arrived at the next destination there would be another, and then another. For we had found that life in the Holy Spirit is a continuous journey, always moving forward. Was everybody here ready for this, or would some be left standing on the platform?

People were ministered to in the vicarage as well, where John and I laid hands on them privately. They came from our churches, and also from the surrounding area as news spread of our ministry. We spent long hours prayer counselling.

One Thursday evening early in March we were helping Evelyn in this way when the telephone rang.

'I'll answer it in the kitchen while you continue,' I called as I hurried from the study to the other end of the house.

My mother's voice greeted me as I picked up the phone. She rarely rang, so I knew something was wrong.

'Is John there with you, dear?' she asked.

'Yes, we're in the middle of counselling somebody,' I replied. 'What are you ringing for at this time of night?'

'I don't know how to say this, Christine.' She sounded distressed. 'Your brother Paul is dead. He died tonight in the swimming baths.'

I stood rooted to the spot. Then I screamed, 'Darling! Darling! Come quickly!'

John came running along the hall. I gave him the phone and clung on weakly to the kitchen table.

'It can't be true,' I thought, 'not again! Once, even twice— but not three times in the same family!'

Paul was my younger brother. At twenty-four he had still been living with my parents at their home. I couldn't understand what had happened. Paul was a strong swimmer, just as Linda had been. I knew that he had not drowned.

My mother explained to John that the police had come and asked my father to identify a body. She told me later that

72

she had said, 'It can't be Paul! He's coming home at half past five. I'm boiling an egg for his tea.'

From somewhere my parents had to find the strength to live a third time through the same nightmare.

That night I lay awake, shocked and upset. I wanted to ask lots of questions and wished that my family were near. I didn't know what to say to the Lord about it in English so I poured it all out in tongues and found a tremendous release. I prayed in tongues all night.

Some of the top specialists in the country gathered at a London hospital with samples from my brother's body. At the end of two days of tests my father was told, 'There is no answer at present. Medical science is not advanced enough to find one.'

The inquest was held about a fortnight later and the verdict given was 'dry drowning'.

Paul was buried in the same grave as his two sisters. As we travelled back to the north after the funeral I felt concerned, especially for my parents, but I just had to leave them in the Lord's hands.

A few weeks later the Lord showed me that I was to rise at six-thirty in the morning and go up into the hills to pray. John didn't mind when I told him, as long as he could stay in bed!

When the alarm rang I slipped out quietly into the beautiful spring morning. The birds were singing as I walked along the road towards Merston, passing several of the factory workers on my way. I nodded and smiled at them.

As I climbed higher into the hills the Lord anointed me, and I felt full of his power. I started to pray aloud and as the Holy Spirit took hold of my words I realized that I was praying a most extraordinary prayer. It arose from a deep desire to be absolutely yielded to the Lord and I gave myself afresh to him.

Then I really longed for him to possess me—not just my heart and mind but, in particular, my body. I asked him to pervade all of it. My fervent desire was that he should possess every component and I found that I was naming each one.

Starting with my hands and feet I covered the outward parts, including my hair and skin. Then there followed a long list of inward organs, like my brain and heart, liver and kidneys—even my muscles and bones. I found myself giving the Lord freedom in parts of my body that I had forgotten were there! These included my metabolism and nervous system, my respiratory and digestive tracts and all my glands. Everything had a mention, however minute it was.

I eventually finished with my arteries, veins and blood and my red and white corpuscles. At the end of the prayer the Lord and I seemed to merge into one in a very awesome experience. The whole episode had been quite incredible and I sank down on to a huge rock to recover. Glancing at my watch I was astonished to see that my prayer had lasted for three hours!

The hills were to become the trysting place where I would frequently meet with the Lord. There he would often speak with me as friend with friend and there I would intercede for many people in need.

Although the Lord had warned me about his power coming upon me in unexpected places I was still surprised when it happened. One day while in the vegetable garden I felt overwhelmed with his love and raised my arms in the air to praise him. The next moment I was flat on my back on the ground. I had a suspicion that he had knocked me over, but got up thinking that I could have fallen. Down I went again! I tried once more, but then I conceded, and just lay there in the long grass basking in the sheer joy of the Lord's presence with me.

When I opened my eyes I caught sight of a double decker bus on the main road the other side of the hedge. The passengers on the top deck had obviously been watching me and all heads were turned backwards, straining to see more as the bus carried them on!

One place where the Lord often chose to come upon me in power was a large supermarket in Huddersfield where John and I purchased our main groceries on days when we travelled the five miles 'to town'.

On the first occasion we were standing by one of the large refrigerators looking for some fish fingers. Suddenly I became aware of a pressure in my solar plexus and I thought that I was going to thump, but instead it pressed me down. I knew that it was the Lord because by now I could recognize when his power was upon me. I clung on to John as I also felt pressure on my head gently forcing me into a crouching position. Then he had the words, 'He that humbles himself shall be exalted.'

'No, Lord, not here!' I giggled, trying to resist. When I failed I pretended to be tying up my shoelace, very aware that other shoppers might be observing my strange behaviour! In fact nobody took any notice.

On the way home we picked up some books from the library and that evening while John was out I started to read one. It was light-hearted fiction and I was soon fully absorbed in the story. But then that still, small voice broke into my reading: 'Put that book down.'

I obeyed.

'Stretch out your hands.'

I did.

'I will use your hands to bless millions.'

'Lord,' I said aloud, 'is this really you? This is the third time I've had this promise in six years. And why me? What about John?' I paused. Then I went on. 'I must be sure about this, Lord. Please will you show me something from the Bible to confirm it?'

Immediately the words 'John 21' were impressed upon my mind. I turned to the chapter and read it right through carefully, but could find nothing significant.

When John came in I shared with him what had happened. He picked up my Bible and began silently reading the chapter.

'What do you mean you can't see anything here?' he asked after a few moments. 'You're wondering whether the promise is truly from the Lord? Well, look at this in verse 7. It says, "It is the Lord". And this is the third time you've had this promise, isn't it? Look at what verse 14 says: "This was now the third time that Jesus was revealed to the disciples after he was raised from the dead.'"

'Oh!' I exclaimd. 'Why didn't I see it?'

'The answer to your other question is here, too,' he went on. 'You've been asking, "What about John?" Well, many people think the disciple whom Jesus especially loved was John. Peter sees him here and says, "Lord, what about this man?" Jesus answers, "What is that to you? (*You*) follow *me*!" The Lord's obviously saying that it doesn't matter at this point what his plan is for me. This is his personal promise to *you*.'

'And I believe that to start with he's calling you to lay hands on people in a wider context than you have done. I suggest you help me in church tomorrow morning.'

So the next day I stood beside John during part of the service and a little nervously embarked upon *my* public healing ministry.

It was natural for me to minister also at the regular parish fellowship meeting in the vicarage lounge. Sometimes no one present was physically sick, but the laying on of hands was offered for any need. In the Scriptures it is used in connection with penitence, assurance, fullness of the Holy Spirit, commissioning and specific blessing, besides healing.

At some of these meetings God's powerful presence could be felt very strongly. One evening, after a period of quiet worship, an awesome stillness descended and we were thrilled with an awareness of the Lord standing right there among us.

'Take off your shoes, for you are standing on holy ground.' The words were spoken through John's lips but it was the God of Moses who was addressing us. We all slipped off our footwear and one by one knelt on the carpet. The prophetic words that followed might have been addressed to any group of believers, and the picture presented was a familiar one, but that night it was just what we needed:

'I am the conductor and you are my orchestra. My desire is to bring out of your lives a beautiful chorus of praise and glory to my name. Each one of you has a particular part to play. Some have more prominent notes to sound than others, but you are all important to me.

'My word to each one of you is to come in when I give you your cue. Do not anticipate this prematurely and make an uncertain sound, neither delay to step out and so miss your opportunity. But be ready to play your part the moment I call upon you.

'To do this you will need to keep your eyes on me. But if you are faithful and obedient to my call I will extract from you a glorious harmony which shall resound far beyond these walls.'

At the close of the meeting the Lord's power was still mightily at work. One lady who had hesitated to ask for ministry found herself being propelled forwards across the room to us by an unseen force. At the same time I found myself gasping for breath, as if struggling against a rushing, mighty wind! The lady stood in front of John and me, and we laid hands on her.

As people left to go home another woman drew me to one side and remarked, 'When you were ministering tonight I saw something like electricity flashing out of your fingers!'

After everyone had gone I lay prostrate on the golden carpet and worshipped again the almighty God who lived with us.

In the years to come I was to experience the same manifestations of power and many others.

It was not long before we were ministering at neighbouring churches as well, taking some of the parish fellowship with us. After John had spoken on healing at the annual meeting of the Baptist deacons in the area we were occasionally invited to minister at services in the chapel at another village.

At the end of one of these services an elderly lady clutching a stick mentioned that she had been too shy to come forward for the laying on of hands.

'Would you like us to pray for you in the vestry?' John asked her.

'Yes, I would,' she replied eagerly.

We ministered to her there for the spinal trouble from which she had suffered for some years.

The next Saturday we took some of our own church

members to the charismatic meeting in Halifax. There a woman stood up to testify and we suddenly realized that she was sharing about the lady with the stick.

'Everyone's talking about it in shops,' she was saying, 'for everybody in village knows her. Her pain's gone and she doesn't need stick any more.'

'Isn't that great!' I whispered to John excitedly.

Pauline was one of the group that we had brought that evening. She had originally come to us for counselling about her marriage problems and God was doing a deep work in her life. She had long blonde hair, and whenever the Lord referred to her in the gifts of the Spirit he called her the fair maiden. One morning he said to us, 'Go and visit the fair maiden in her home.'

When we got there Pauline was very distressed. She was in agony with a trapped nerve in her neck.

'The doctor's just been,' she explained, 'and he's given me a prescription for some pain killers. But now that the Lord's sent you as well perhaps you'll minister to me.'

We had begun the practice of sometimes laying our hands on the affected part of a person's body, so while we prayed for Pauline I laid my hands on her neck.

A few days later when we saw Pauline again she was enthusiastically waving the prescription at us.

'I didn't need this after all!' she said delightedly.

For several years afterwards Pauline would bring out her prescription as evidence of how Jesus had healed her and would use the opportunity to talk about him.

Another instant healing occurred in church one morning. A middle-aged man who had had a hernia for some time came up for ministry. He went down in the Spirit and when he picked himself up off the floor the hernia had completely receded.

There was a mixed reaction among the church members to reports of these healings. While some were rejoicing, others were apathetic.

The Lord pinpointed the different attitudes at another service: 'Some of you are like hedgehogs. As soon as I begin to move among you you curl up into a ball. Some are like rabbits. At the sound of my voice you scamper away into your burrows. Others are like flowers. You welcome what I am doing, and are attractive to those who pass by, but you stay in the same place all the time. Others are what I desire you all to be: like birds, soaring free and flying high with me.'

With all that was happening we had almost forgotten the prophecy about the axe. But in a subtle way it had already begun to hack at us. Soon we would feel the full force of its cutting power.

8

A Black Cloud Above Us

Everyone had received communion and John was placing the vessels down when he felt an unnatural warmth in his right ear. Simultaneously he knew that he was to prophesy:

'The Lord is saying that we are not to believe all that we hear with our outward ears. He would have us claim the victory over idle and malicious gossip and he will unblock ears to receive the truth. He who has an ear, let him hear.'

Such gossip was already increasing, especially among those who resented the ministry. But from that time on the Lord would warn us when this was happening, for he would give John that same warmth in his ear, and when he did we claimed the victory in Jesus' name. On more than one occasion we discovered details afterwards which proved that gossip was going on at the exact time that we had prayed.

By now several newcomers had joined us at Merston Mill church, and because they had come to know Jesus through our ministry they naturally supported us. But there were other people who were beginning to resist the laying on of hands.

I was very aware of this as I stood at the front to minister. At this point in the service I usually seemed to fill up with power. Sometimes it could be quite painful. As I ministered and discharged this power I was left with another pain: that of knowing that the ministry was being rejected by some. John is not as sensitive to atmospheres as I am and at first he was unaware of the hostility directed at us. But it was soon made plain to him in the vestry one morning after the service, when a youngish man openly voiced the criticisms.

'We've no objection to you doing your healing, John,' he said condescendingly, 'it's your *style* we don't like. Why put on a show? Can't it be doon on quiet? And this falling down, you ought to do away with that.'

'Well,' John responded, 'I can only minister in the way the Lord leads me. We do lay hands on people in private, but he's been leading us to minister in public in the church and we don't wish to limit the Holy Spirit. Aren't you pleased about those who've received healing and blessing since we've been here?'

The man ignored the question. 'Soom of us have been here for years and have doon well enough without all this,' he stated flatly.

John nodded sympathetically. 'I appreciate it takes time to get used to something new, and some are moving at a faster pace than others. But my concern is for everybody, not just the people belonging to the churches. I'm responsible for all who live in the two parishes. They need to know that Jesus is alive and still at work today.'

'Oh!' said the man abruptly. 'Evangelism! We have soom-one in church who has gift for that. We leave that to him. We've enough of us own problems to sort out before we get involved with outsiders.'

John stared at him, a little bewildered.

'It's not just one person's job to evangelize!' he started to explain. But the man had had his say and was off.

In the months following, many similar conversations took place. There were only a few hostile people but somehow they managed to influence a number of others. At first they questioned our ministries, then began to oppose them. When as a result protests or criticisms were brought to John he patiently explained what he believed the Lord wanted.

But as the blessings and healings increased, so did the opposition.

One night just as we were about to go to sleep I saw a big

black cloud in my mind. I shared this with John.

'It's over Merston Mill church!' I exclaimed with dismay as I saw it hovering menacingly. 'It looks as if it could break at any moment!'

I felt fear clutching at my mind and snuggled up into John's arms. 'I do wish we hadn't come here!' I cried desperately.

John was also inwardly worried, but he tried to comfort me as we drifted off to sleep.

The next day things seemed brighter and when John returned from an afternoon's visiting he was in high spirits again.

'Guess what!' he said, pouring himself a cup of tea. 'I've had a boiling hot foot this afternoon, similar to when I have a hot ear. But I don't know what it means.'

'I do!' I said with a laugh. 'The Lord wants you to pray for Joe. He's had a bad foot for ages now. Don't you remember how I used to get my thumb when the Lord wanted me to pray for you?' John had suffered in the past with a painful thumb and my thumb hurting had been a signal to pray for him.

Another sign which God used was pressure on my nose. Whenever I felt this I was directed to pray for a certain man who had had an operation on his nose.

The Lord eventually built up quite a large number of supernatural signs which we learned to interpret. He used our bodies—and particularly mine—like a code. Sometimes, for example, if he wanted to say 'no' to something, I would find my head shaking, or perhaps my eyes closing, or even my foot stamping. Another way he showed us that we were not to do something was by gently pushing me backwards. Just like the thumps, these signs frequently came when we were least expecting them.

At first we were suspicious of them, but as they kept coming they proved to be true and valuable. When the Lord chose this miming procedure to guide us, we could ascertain whom to contact and what to pray for, where to go and what to do and how to proceed if we were unsure. But at other times when we needed guidance no signs came. For these signs only occurred every so often. We learned to rely on the inner witness of the Holy Spirit, and not on the signs, helpful though they were.

One afternoon John and I were sitting again beside the waterfall. This had become one of our favourite spots for talking things out. We began to discuss how the Lord had been speaking to us recently and I asked John, 'Are there any incidents in the Bible where the Lord speaks in similar ways?'

'Yes,' he replied slowly, 'I think there are. The Israelites had Urim and Thummim, a supernatural indication on the high priests breastplate that showed which way God wanted them to proceed. And some prophets did stranger things than you've done! Ezekiel ate a scroll, drew a map on a brick, dug through a wall, and all sorts of other actions to signify God's will. Then in the New Testament we find Agabus taking Paul's girdle and binding his hands and feet with it to signify the danger the apostle would be in if he went to Jerusalem.'

'Oh!' I exclaimed. 'But I wonder why it happens to *me* so much? Do you think it has anything to do with that extraordinary prayer I prayed? You know, when I first went up to the hills. I told you about it. I gave God access to every part of my body.'

'It seems very likely,' agreed my husband.

'And there's the prayer I prayed when I was baptized in the Spirit,' I added. 'I asked God to show me in a tangible way that he was real, and ever since then he's been giving me physical manifestations of his presence.'

'Yes,' John said quietly, 'and I've an idea it's because the Lord's preparing you for something more.' He looked into my eyes. 'It might be years before it comes to fruition, though.' He squeezed my hand and looked at his watch. 'Let's get back home! I'd better get ready for the meeting tonight.'

That night John went off to the meeting with a smile on his face but when he returned he looked sad and drained. This was becoming a usual occurrence and it concerned me. The opposition to our ministries appeared to be turning into something more like an organized persecution of the vicar.

I had once attended a business meeting and had been amazed at the behaviour of some of the people there towards my husband. Mainly it was coming from just a few, but the false accusations were brought up subtly and had obviously been prepared beforehand. At that meeting John had been accused of being authoritarian, of pushing his ministry upon people and of going to too many meetings outside the parish.

My ministry was also being questioned, for I was doing it when I had not been ordained! Some church members even wrote letters of complaint about us to the bishop.

I watched my husband's reactions as these and other concerns became magnified out of all proportion. Throughout he remained calm and dignified, always polite as he gently endeavoured to put right the false assumptions. My heart ached for him, and I felt so helpless. But at times his face shone and I knew that the Lord was with him.

As time passed, hostility was expressed in a different way —that of non-cooperation. John sometimes arrived at Merston Mill church to find nothing prepared for the service. Or he would come back to the church after taking a service at Wilfirth to find nothing cleared away.

People who had agreed to do responsible tasks stopped doing them without warning, so John began to give them to some of the newcomers. But this upset some of the people who had been going there for years. One Sunday I arrived in church to find no flowers there, so I dashed out to the vicarage garden and hastily gathered some.

John was also refused any increase in his expense allowance, so once again we were forced to use the house-keeping money on petrol and other essential items which he needed for his work in the parish.

However, there were many that stood by us and also a good number of the congregation who looked on, apparently unable to make much sense of what was happening. Meanwhile, at Wilfirth the work continued generally peacefully

and steadily. The very different congregation there seemed
to be fairly appreciative of John's ministry.

During the holiday period there were very few worshippers
at the Merston Mill family service as most of the factory
workers went away at the same time. On one particular
morning as we were few in number we gathered for the
service in the choir stalls at the front of the church. There was
a terrible atmosphere, and when we came to the period of the
laying on of hands an uneasy silence fell. As John and I stood
waiting to minister I sensed the Lord's power about to
descend. Almost at the same time John began to prophesy:
'What if I were to come back now? Would you all be ready? Is
this how I wish to find you? Will you not return to me and
accept the authority and ministries which I have placed
among you? What if I were to come back now?'

The power coming from these words was taking my breath
away. Then I heard a loud thud. It was my head hitting the
stone chancel floor! When I got up I felt like a rag. I had to sit
for the remainder of the service, but felt totally relaxed and
was completely unhurt.

Sometimes during the sharing of God's peace in a communion service John would encourage people to go towards
one another, and many resentments appeared to melt away
as Christians embraced or shook hands in the name of the
Lord. However, at this point one couple always seemed to
have a sudden urge to kneel and pray!

After one service this same couple and others started
shouting abuse at my husband in the church car park. People
standing by tried to reason with them, but John listened
calmly without retaliating. This annoyed his opponents even
more. When they found that they were getting nowhere they
stamped around the drive waving their arms wildly in the
air. After that they climbed into their cars and drove off, still
shouting loudly and shaking their fists at us. We stood there
watching, absolutely flabbergasted.

'I've never seen adult people behaving in such a childish
manner!' I remarked to John. 'Whatever next?'

'Well, I was hoping for some lunch,' he said tentatively,

turning towards the vicarage.

Later, as we were doing the washing up together, the hurt which had been building up inside me began to surface. I was finding it hard to watch the man I loved being attacked so venomously.

'Can't you see, darling, what these people are trying to do?' I asked angrily. 'They don't want your ministry, so in their own way they're trying to force you out.'

'That's not right!' John retorted crossly. 'You know that some here have benefited greatly through what we've done. I could give you a long list of them and there must be others that we don't know of as well.'

I stared out of the kitchen window at the cows grazing on the hills in the distance.

'Out there somewhere,' I said, raising my voice, 'there are thousands of people who long to know that Jesus is real.' My temper was rising. 'They *want* what we have to give. I know that some here do, but mainly I think you're running a religious club. Yes,' (I was shouting now) 'a club for people just interested in religion, who don't really want to be disturbed by the living God!'

I sat down, exhausted by my outburst and John stormed out of the kitchen, slamming the door behind him.

But in the middle of our troubles the Lord still encouraged us. One lady decided to put into practice a slogan that she had seen on our mantlepiece in the lounge: 'Expect a miracle'. The result for her was a brand new home, a job which she had been looking for, and the return of her estranged son from America. She was thrilled, and wrote to tell us so.

More encouragement came through words at the parish fellowship: 'I want you to feel my love tonight. I am coming to soothe and refresh each one of you by dabbing you all over as it were with soft cotton wool.'

'At this time the sky overhead is black, but there will come a time when blue skies will be above you again. These in turn will change into red skies, for I will display my power in this area.'

'Springs of water are rising from a dry and parched land.

Here and there throughout this region they have begun to spring up. Soon there will be more, and the waters will increase until there is a mighty flood.'

Some Christians were given pictures in their homes to share with us for our encouragement. Each person approached us separately, unaware that they were confirming what others had seen.

'You are going to have a big ministry,' said one, 'I saw you both in front of crowds of people.'

'The Lord showed me a map,' said another. 'Your ministry is going to be worldwide.'

Someone else saw us boarding a plane with John carrying a big Bible.

Yet another person shared, 'I saw you both on a stage, and there were hundreds of people. They seemed to be of different races.'

We praised the Lord for his assurance and felt excited. We had learned, though, not to speculate about how such prophecies might come to pass.

One morning a young woman called Gloria came to coffee. John's original contact with her had been through her baby's baptism. As a result she had come back to the Lord and joined the church.

'That girl needs deliverance!' I said to John after she had left. 'She has evil spirits in her.'

'You make the most ridiculous statements at times,' joked my husband, 'but I have to admit you're usually right in the end! You remember what one woman said to you soon after we moved here? "I can see there's no point in hiding anything from you. You can see right through me!"'

'That's all very well,' I replied, 'but it's a lonely experience being able to detect what others can't see, invaluable though it is.'

Later Gloria freely admitted her involvement in spiritism and the occult. She also shared that she had been overtaken sometimes by trances. However, she wanted to be set free and arrangements were made for her deliverance.

While praying beforehand about this I felt my face harden.

'What can it mean?' I asked John.

'Well, the only thing I can think of is when Jesus set his face like a flint to go to Jerusalem,' he replied thoughtfully.

'I feel sure I have to fast,' I said. Later we realized that the sign meant that I should be determined to see the fast through.

I had already discovered the value of fasting. Usually I cut out all food but drank normally. I found that this enhanced my mind, enabling me to receive clearer guidance. But on a three day fast I was always tempted to give up at the end of the second day. I needed persistence with the fast for Gloria as it lasted for four days, the whole of the duration of our ministry to her.

Several of us were involved in this, and we were shown that 'through praise shall the victory come'. We saw how Satan hates it when we praise God, and as the spirits in Gloria reacted to our worship and manifested themselves we cast them out in the name of Jesus. As each one left I experienced an identical release in my own body. One of them would not budge while being addressed in English but left rapidly when spoken to in a tongue! At one point Gloria shook violently as the evil spirits within her trembled while they listened to us reading the Scriptures about Satan's final doom.

After two days we came to a halt. We knew that Gloria was not completely free but we could get no further. So we rang a friend in London and explained our problem.

'Have you cut her free from her ancestral line?' he enquired. 'You remember that in Exodus it states, "The sins of the fathers are visited upon the children to the third and fourth generation"? Well, it may be that these particular spirits have a hold on Gloria because of what she's inherited from her ancestors. If you set her free from them you may find that you can proceed.'

'Thanks,' John said gratefully. 'We'll try it.' We did, and found that it worked.

The way was now clear for complete deliverance. But even then the last spirit tried to pretend that it was not there! We were sure that it was, for the Lord had also built up a code with us in this realm.

Finally John had a picture of a suitcase being shut down tightly and firmly locked, and the words, 'The case is closed'. We all knew that it was and praised the Lord for what he had done.

We had learned so much during these four days. But we find that deliverance cases vary. We can gain from our past experiences but it is important each time to be led step by step by the Holy Spirit.

After the summer holidays the demands and pressures upon John in particular accelerated rapidly. He spent so much time during the day dealing with people that much of his preparation and paperwork was pushed to late in the evening.

When he eventually got to bed it was still all going around in his mind. He also felt torn inside by a conflict of loyalties: to his family, his parishes, his bishop, the people who stood by him, the ones who were demanding changes in his ministry and above all to the Lord and his calling.

He wondered constantly what the outcome of all the trouble would be. The responsibility lay heavily upon him and the more that he tried to see a way out the more it eluded him. His mind began to race and his body was denied the sleep which he so badly needed.

9

The Day Our World Collapsed

Soon the broken nights turned into completely sleepless
ones. During the night before the Harvest Festival a torrent
of pictures raced through John's mind. They were jumbled
and made no sense and he felt alarmed. The fact that he was
unable to control them frightened him and he sat bolt upright
in bed.

'For goodness' sake try and get some sleep!' I said drowsily.
'What are you sitting up for in the middle of the night?'

John lay back down, but tossed and turned until daylight.

Merston Mill church looked beautiful for the harvest and
was packed for the morning service. But at lunch time John
was absolutely exhausted and he could not even muster the
strength to lift his knife and fork.

'I don't feel like eating,' he said weakly, 'I'll have to go to
bed for an hour.' I was not surprised, in view of his recent
sleepless nights. I marvelled that he had taken the service so
well and preached such an excellent sermon.

'We'll go for a walk when you get up,' I said cheerfully,
taking away his unwanted meal.

But John discovered that he couldn't sleep. His mind was
far too alert. The walk might have done him some good, but
it had to be cut short as he had an appointment at the
vicarage with a woman who had asked for his help.

Maisie was one of those people whom the healing ministry
attracts. She had many problems, mental, emotional and

spiritual. She spent her time going to different sources to gain help, but didn't appear to improve.

Having travelled a long way for ministry she stayed on for the evening service. I noticed that although the church was fairly full she chose a whole pew near the front to herself. I sat on the left hand side of the church opposite her and the boys sat in the pew in front of me with their friends.

As the service progressed I heard some peculiar noises coming regularly from Maisie's pew. She was burping very loudly, over and over again. Stephen and Paul started giggling. I poked them in the back.

'Be quiet!' I whispered. But as the burping continued I could see their shoulders shaking as they desperately endeavoured to control their mirth.

Meanwhile, John was taking the service as if nothing unusual was happening. I could see that he had chosen to ignore Maisie, which I thought was wise as she was obviously seeking attention.

By the time that we came to the second scripture reading she was lying fully outstretched on the pew, talking loudly. The visiting preacher, who was reading the lesson, had to shout to make his voice heard above her. But as he did this Maisie raised her voice even more. So then he read louder still! Obviously something would have to be done about her.

So when the reading had finished John announced a hymn, and while everyone was singing Maisie was led to the front. John rebuked Satan in the name of Jesus and the power of God hit her. She sank to the floor and remained there a while. Then she got up like a lamb and was silent for the rest of the service.

Afterwards John had yet another harvest service to take, at the local cricket club. When he came home it was late, but there were still a few of us in the kitchen drinking coffee. I was surprised when he walked straight past me without giving me any greeting.

I could see that there was something strange about him and when we went to bed I began to get really worried. For not only did John not sleep but he kept taking non-stop throughout the night. He seemed unable to cope with the barrage of thoughts rushing through his mind. He started throwing out questions at me, vainly endeavouring to find some explanation for his confusion. But I was tired and found his constant chatter wearing.

'Let's get some sleep,' I pleaded, 'We'll talk about it tomorrow.'

'I've seen him overtired before,' I thought, 'but it never affected him like this.'

John's incessant talking continued all through the next day. In the afternoon we went over to the church to sort out the harvest gifts for the sick and elderly. But he found it difficult to concentrate and kept walking around restlessly. As we returned to the house he asked suspiciously, 'Is that noise someone's radio?'

'What noise?' I said, bewildered. 'I can't hear anything.'

Later that evening I was really embarrassed while distributing the gifts at a local old people's home.

'That old woman over there!' John said loudly. 'She's winking at me!'

'Sssh!' I whispered. 'Don't be ridiculous!'

In spite of these worrying signs it didn't occur to me that there was anything seriously wrong with him, only that he was overwrought. But as soon as we went to bed he started firing questions at me again. This time his eyes were blazing and his manner frightening.

'They're after me!' he exclaimed suddenly, his face pale with fear.

'Who? The people who don't like your ministry? They can't harm you!'

'Not just them!' he snapped back. 'Everyone's after me!' He pointed at me accusingly. 'You could even be one of them!'

Then he questioned me viciously, apparently trying to discover whether I really was his wife! I was absolutely terrified and jumped out of bed while he continued his tirade.

'Will he turn violent?' I wondered. We were alone with the boys in the house and I felt very vulnerable. So though it was the middle of the night I rang Joe and Evelyn. I spoke to them both for a few minutes and they helped to calm me.

Uneasily I climbed back into bed and tried to sleep but it was difficult with my husband's voice rambling on in the background. Eventually I dozed off just as morning was dawning.

That day the doctor was called.

'My husband's had no sleep recently,' I explained. I felt that if only John could get some sleep he would be all right.

But after the doctor had listened intently to John he told him kindly, 'I know a specialist who can help you. I'll bring him to see you tomorrow. Meanwhile, I'll give you some tablets. They'll help you to sleep and calm you down.'

The following day John took to his bed. 'I have pains all over my body,' he complained. 'I feel really ill.'

When I took his lunch up he stared at it. Then he shouted, 'I can't eat that! You're trying to poison me!'

I looked at him in amazement.

'Don't be silly!' I said nervously. 'Come on, eat it up. You need it for strength.'

The doctor returned and brought with him a psychiatrist. They stayed with John for a long time and then they asked to see me privately. We went into the study and our doctor spoke in a solemn voice: 'Mrs Huggett, your husband is seriously ill. He's suffering from a mental breakdown. We must get him away from the parish for a complete rest.'

I was astonished.

'I had no idea!' I said quietly.

It had all appeared to happen so suddenly. But breakdowns are often rooted in childhood, and nowadays when we pray for people with depressive illness we ask the Lord to go back in time to when they were young.

Occasionally in the past John had suffered from nervous exhaustion, and once, at Buckhurst Hill, he had been ordered by the doctor to take a few days' holiday. Although he had put on a brave face during the recent traumas they had been the last straw and had done him far more damage than either of us had suspected. If only we had recognized the warning signs!

93

As we all trooped back into the bedroom John asked anxiously, 'What's wrong with me, doctor?'

'You are in an acute anxiety state,' explained the psychiatrist. 'I'll be in touch with your bishop to see if we can get you away for a break.'

A day or two later our doctor came back to find out how John was. By then the tablets had achieved their desired effect. He had calmed down and we had been able to sleep. He was talking more sensibly and was anxious to know how quickly he could be well again.

The doctor explained: 'What's happened is that the chemicals in your brain have become out of balance. In time they should right themselves again, but until they do you will need to be on tranquillizers.'

'I know I've been suffering from paranoia,' said John despondently, 'but I cannot seem to shake it off. I'm getting worried about going away now, as well.'

'That's part of the illness, too. But you must get away from the phone and from all the interruptions here.'

The bishop arranged for John to stay at a private hospital in York, fifty miles away. A week later I drove him there and a friend accompanied us.

I watched John being subjected to the initial admission procedure. Everyone was very kind but I shared in his humiliation as they stripped him of everything and started sewing name tags on his clothes.

Suddenly it dawned on me what was happening to my highly intelligent, articulate husband. He had always been so much in command of every situation, but now circumstances had overtaken him. My heart ached for him. I bit my lip.

'I mustn't cry when I say goodbye,' I thought stoically, 'I don't want him to see how upset I am.'

When the time arrived it was hard and I was grateful to have my friend to chat with on the way home.

Meanwhile, John had been ushered into a dormitory which, in spite of the generally plush nature of the hospital, reminded him of an army barrack room.

First he had had the shock of realizing that he was in a psychiatric establishment and then the humiliation of being stripped of all his clothes and personal belongings. He later learned that the nurses didn't dare to leave even keys or coins on patients, in case any of them attempted violence or suicide.

John's third shock was having to remain, for the first two days, in the one room, wearing only a dressing gown. Just as in the army, he was also subjected to a radical haircut! He felt like a prisoner.

On the second evening he was allowed into the recreation room and as he played snooker with another patient John suddenly felt elated. But it was short-lived.

'It must be the tablets they've given me,' he thought disappointedly as his anxieties quickly returned.

The following morning he was allowed out of his dormitory and told that from then on he must only sleep there. He was free now to talk to others and take part in specific activities. But everywhere he went he was accompanied by the confusing and sometimes horrifying pictures in his mind.

'If I could just settle to doing something, perhaps they would go away,' he thought wistfully, 'but I'm too tense.' He attempted to watch television but his sense of hearing had intensified and he couldn't bear it for long.

Soon he found that his condition was affecting his body again, and he began to cry out in pain. His whole body hurt and he felt weak and breathless. A young man was standing in the corridor, looking on sympathetically.

'Try taking a bath,' he urged. 'That sometimes helps.' John took his advice and experienced temporary relief.

But whatever he did he could not eradicate the fears in his mind. He started talking incessantly to the nurses. They listened patiently and this helped a little.

He also began to notice some of the other patients there as they too shared their troubles. There were several other professional people in his wing, including a teacher, a Roman Catholic priest, and a doctor named Godfrey. One meal time John sat next to Godfrey.

'I did a silly thing,' the doctor confided. 'I was so tired

from night calls that I took barbiturates to keep myself awake. And when I mixed them with alcohol they blew my mind.'

John felt sorry for him and began telling him how his own breakdown had occurred.

'Of course,' remarked Godfrey casually, 'this place is like a prison to escape from. I know people who've been here for years.'

John felt alarmed. He left the table uneasily.

'*I* don't want to stay here that long!' he thought fearfully.

News spreads fast in villages, and various snippets of gossip about John soon reached my ears. A favourite was, 'They've had to take vicar away.' Another was, 'She's going to have a job with him for the rest of her life.' So much ignorance still exists about mental illness!

Life became busier than ever at the vicarage. It was some time before I managed to undo all the arrangements which John had made for the coming weeks. Some events, like the harvest supper for the parish fellowship, could still go ahead. Everything had to be worked around my daily trip to York and back. The children required extra attention as well, because they were caught up in something that they didn't fully understand.

Each day I visited John he seemed to be worse. Heavily drugged, and walking around like a zombie, he didn't look like my husband. My times with him consisted of listening to a lot of nonsense. His grip on reality had gone. On the first weekend I took the boys to see him but he ignored them. As we drove home I was heartbroken.

'He's not the man I married any more!' I thought despairingly. 'I've just visited a complete stranger. I wonder whether he'll ever be right again?' I felt literally sick with worry.

My thoughts were abruptly interrupted.

'Look out!' Stephen shouted.

I braked hard, but I could see that we were going to hit a car that was already on the roundabout which we were entering fast. Deep in my thoughts of despair I had failed to pull up at the give way sign. There was a loud bang as we crashed head on into the side of the other vehicle.

I was surprised to find that I was still alive and breathed a quick prayer of thanks. Hastily I turned to check on the boys, both of whom were in the back seat. Stephen had blood pouring from a six inch gash in his forehead. Paul's chest had taken a hammering against the front seat.

'Oh no!' I cried. 'I'm sorry!' I felt personally responsible for their injuries.

The couple from the other car joined us. I looked up.

'Are you all right?' I gasped. 'It was totally my fault.' The man nodded, handing me a handkerchief to help mop up the blood. People from nearby houses ran out with towels and water.

The ambulance arrived and we were taken to a hospital in Leeds. Stephen was stitched up and Paul examined and then we were discharged. I was unharmed except for a wrenched pelvis.

A policewoman took me aside and warned me that at a later date I would be charged with careless driving. But that was the least of my concerns just then. I was wondering how we were going to get home.

But we had two good friends in Joe and Evelyn. The hospital authorities rang them and they came to fetch us. I learnt later that the car was a 'write-off', and was horrified when Joe took me to see it.

'How did we come out of it alive?' I exclaimed. 'The Lord certainly protected us.'

Joe helped me search through John's files until we found the car insurance policy. There were forms to fill in and diagrams to draw.

'I could have done without all this!' I thought. 'Where's it all going to end?'

Back at York John was dimly aware that he was getting worse. He walked about as though in a dream, slightly suspicious of everyone, unsure if he could trust them.

Anxiety pervaded his whole life. He was anxious if I happened to be late in visiting him. He was worried about seeing the psychiatrist. When one event passed he simply transferred his anxiety on to something else.

When I visited him next I tried to explain about the car crash but his interest was only momentary. He was unable to enter into what I was having to cope with. This was utterly unlike the man that I used to know.

One day John attempted some occupational therapy, but he had never been very adept with his hands and he soon gave up. His coordination was worse than ever. Even writing his signature became an effort. He had been used to playing the piano and tried to play it again, but without success. The crowning humiliation came one lunchtime when he just could not coordinate his hand movements, and a nurse had to feed him like a young child.

Only one week had passed, but it seemed like a year and each day he longed for bedtime when the drugged sleep would bring relief to his pained body and disturbed mind.

Some mornings he walked alone in the hospital grounds. The fresh air was good to breathe. Nature in all its autumn loveliness seemed strangely attractive and he felt a drawing towards the outdoors that he had never experienced before. He gazed at the flowers one day, and was impressed by the sheer brilliance and beauty of their colours.

'I've missed so much of your lovely creation, Lord,' he said regretfully, and he began to praise God in tongues. As he did so he felt an inward release and the knowledge that although the Lord appeared to be silent he was still with him.

On returning indoors he was met by a lady social worker who was a Christian.

'There's a clergyman friend of mine wishing to see you,' she said, smiling at him.

An elderly gentleman greeted John lovingly and listened while he poured out his fears.

'God has been so close to me in the past,' my husband said quietly, 'but now he seems so far away. My fears and anxieties appear to have swamped his reality.'

They continued to converse and then the visiting clergyman offered to minister the laying on of hands which John gladly accepted.

'If only I were at home,' my husband thought longingly. 'I could receive ministry like this every day!' He realized how much he was missing his Christian friends and most of all he yearned to be at home again with me.

But even if he did get home soon how could he go back into such an unpleasant church situation? And could he cope with it?

10

'Follow the Candle'

'I want him out, doctor,' I said firmly, 'this place is making
him worse!'

The psychiatrist stared hard at me and there was silence
for a moment. He adjusted his spectacles and glanced down
at the notes on his desk.

'Do you think you will be able to cope?' he asked gravely.

'I think so. He's not likely to turn violent, is he?'

'No, your problem would be his unpredictability.'

'I'll manage,' I said resolutely.

So, after a fortnight away, John was allowed to come
home. Joe took me to collect him and even on the way back I
wondered if I had made a wise decision.

'Look!' John exclaimed timorously, pointing to a signpost.
'They're trying to confuse us. The sign for West Yorkshire
has been moved!'

Joe and I exchanged meaningful looks and quickly started
chatting about something else.

But when we arrived back at the vicarage I realized that
my troubles had only just begun. My husband was like a
young child to cope with. Although very soon the persecution
complex, the pains and the disturbing pictures all disappeared, his anxieties remained. I was giving of myself constantly to him and I soon felt very frustrated.

Our friends called to encourage him—mainly members of
the parish fellowship, which continued to meet in our house.

100

But he was unable to reciprocate in any way.

In November we held the parish weekend, which was led by a visiting preacher. John made his own presence very conspicuous at this by drawing attention to his ailments at every available opportunity, though he could not last out the full length of any session. It was beginning to look very unlikely that he would be able to return to fulltime parochial work after Christmas as he had hoped.

Alongside his incessant talking came a total dependence upon me. He always had to have someone with him, for if he was left alone with his anxieties he was terrified. This meant that if I wanted to go out without him one of our friends had to act as a 'babysitter'.

The cold wintry days began to drag as our once hectic life in the parish diminished. There was a big gap on Sundays especially, so we decided to go out each weekend as a family. I thought that this would help with John's rehabilitation, but he was still living in a dream world and was a real encumbrance. The drugs had slowed him down so much that he couldn't even walk at the same pace as the rest of us.

Sometimes he would relate in great detail the reasons why he could not participate in activities. He went on and on, and it was impossible to reason with him. His mind was still unbalanced and his thinking illogical. Often he picked on one word, twisting its original meaning and magnifying its implications. I found that the best method of treating him at this stage was to humour him, though my patience wore a bit thin at times.

After Christmas John was able to tag along with me when I went shopping. One morning he made a fuss outside the large supermarket.

'I'm going to faint! Quick, help me!'

This was the latest complaint, a feeling that he could not breathe. But I knew that it was entirely a product of his mind, and I deliberately walked on into the shop, ignoring him. He soon followed but after a while he became disorientated and rushed out.

Similar scenes occurred several times. It didn't matter

where we were or whom we were with. He was definitely unpredictable.

One day a group of us were in deep conversation in the study. John was with us, looking quite subdued. Then suddenly he shouted, 'I'm going to collapse! I'm going to die!'

I felt so exasperated by then that I just said ruefully, 'If you are going to die I do wish you would hurry up and get on with it! You've said it so many times.' I knew that he couldn't help it but I felt as if I was being worn away. I was summoning all my wits to anticipate which tactic to use for the next onslaught.

I felt incredibly alone. I tried to help the boys understand that their father was ill. But they couldn't grasp the situation and as they watched his bizarre behaviour they gradually lost all respect for him. Friends prayed and tried to support me but they could only help in a very limited way.

I also felt very discouraged and wondered whether this man that I loved would ever be like he used to be. Sometimes, while he was still asleep in the morning, I shut myself in the spare bedroom and sobbed and sobbed before the Lord.

As I poured it all out to him the realization gradually dawned upon me that nothing else really mattered except my relationship with Jesus. If that was right I could be stripped of everything and it would merely reveal that he was my all in all. Not only did I find that he was totally and absolutely sufficient but I experienced an even deeper unity with him than before.

Soon the time drew near for my appearance in court at Leeds.

'How does it feel to have a criminal among the clergy wives in your diocese?' I asked the bishop jokingly.

'Is John going with you?' he enquired.

'Yes,' I replied.

'I'll meet you both there,' he said.

'What a kind gesture!' I thought happily. 'The bishop has been so good to us in practical ways throughout John's illness.'

When the day arrived, all three of us stood in a busy

corridor for about an hour before it was my turn to go in. As we filed into the courtroom we must have presented an interesting spectacle: first me, then John in his clerical collar, followed by the bishop in his.

The charge was driving without due care and attention and I was asked if I wished to say anything. I told them of the worrying circumstances which surrounded the accident. The magistrates listened sympathetically but explained that, as I had broken the law, there was no alternative except to fine me. Before leaving I paid the fine in full and was glad to have the whole episode behind me.

Gradually John improved. But it was very slowly and he was unable to work full-time yet. The incessant talking period had lasted for several months. After that he entered on a different stage. He was exceptionally silent for most of the time. I spent much emotional energy in attempting to converse with him. I longed for him to come towards me and the children in some way, but he just could not.

Instead he would look across longingly at the church, waiting for the time when he could return to the work. But I couldn't understand why he wanted to go back, after all that had happened.

In February we had a holiday at Mabledon again. While there we travelled to see the Dearings, and they took us out for a meal. Before we left them we prayed together and Trevor had these words for us from the Lord: 'Follow the candle'. We were grateful for the promise of a little light, even if it was just to be like a candle flickering.

When we arrived back at Mabledon we prayed about the candle and what it meant. For the first time for a long period the Lord spoke through John: 'When you are in the dark holding a candle you can only see the immediate surroundings. That is all that you can see at the moment. When the candle moves, follow it. You will only see a little at a time, but I shall guide you like this until you emerge from the dark rooms into the light.'

After returning to Yorkshire John occasionally had two or three days at a time when he was more like his old self. It was evident that, although the clay had been smashed, the potter had begun to put the pieces together again.

So when John next visited the psychiatrist he was quite unprepared for what he was told.

'I advise you,' the doctor said frankly, 'not to take on again the responsibilities you had in those two parishes. It would involve you in further conflict. Perhaps you could look for a post elsewhere?'

John was shocked and at first he was very upset.

'It's as if the people against me have won!' he thought dismally.

However, after he had told me about the doctor's advice I felt as if a great burden had been lifted.

When we prayed about it the Lord reminded us very clearly that it was *his* ministry, not John's and therefore *he* would be the one to vindicate us. This promise of vindication came continually, though we found it difficult to envisage how it could happen now that John, though still the vicar, no longer fulfilled the duties of a parish priest.

As time went on he continued to receive counselling and ministry from various Christians. He was determined to discover the root cause of his breakdown so that the Lord could deal with it completely. Very gently God brought things to the surface so that they could be lifted right out of him.

One blustery March morning, while John was out walking alone, he was suddenly overwhelmed with a sense of guilt and failure.

'How I've let you down, Lord!' he cried out in his heart. 'I've honestly tried to do what you wanted but I've failed in so many ways. And look how I've ended up! I've been so proud, Lord, and now my ministry's collapsed. And you had promised us so much more!'

Wearily he sat down on one of the rugged stone walls, and found that he was repenting of one thing after another. It was like a purging and afterwards he felt refreshed. Deep down inside him some wrong attitudes had been unearthed and cleansed away.

When John returned home we praised the Lord together and he spoke to us about our future: 'You must be patient. I have prepared a way for you. Fear not, follow the candle. The road will have many twists and turns but I will bring you safely through.'

During the months that followed we certainly needed patience. We thought that perhaps a team ministry would be the answer, so that John could share the burden of responsibility with other clergy. But after applying to one or two we couldn't muster any enthusiasm for them.

In spite of our circumstances people still came to us asking for ministry. I was forced to take the lead in this as John was so silent. He could, however, lay hands on people with me and would sometimes give an appropriate word from the Lord.

We were also reading more books at this time and in doing so we discovered another dimension of healing, 'soaking prayer'.

Francis McNutt, in his book *The Power to Heal*, shares what we had already experienced, that one short prayer is often insufficient for complete healing. The person frequently requires a course of treatment, especially when the condition is long-term or serious.

The author's concept of soaking prayer was that of laying hands on the affected part for long periods, so that the healing energy could 'soak in'. He had found that some physical conditions clearly improved after a short session of laying on of hands, and it was these which responded far more when soaking prayer was applied.

John and I could see that this made sense, and were eager to put it into practice. Independently of each other, the Lord showed us the person with whom we were to start. His name was Albert, and he had been seriously injured during the second world war. He and his wife Freda were members of Merston Mill church. They gladly welcomed the prospect of our ministering in this way after we had explained to them exactly what it entailed. So, with some trepidation, we entered into the realm of soaking prayer.

We arranged an evening once a week which we could give fully to Albert and Freda in their home. When we arrived there the first time, we didn't know how to proceed, so we began by placing our hands on Albert's spine, where he was most seriously injured, and waiting upon the Lord. Step by step the Holy Spirit guided us.

Each week the procedure varied. Sometimes Albert would lie outstretched on the floor while we kept our hands on his back for periods of half an hour or more. During this we might praise the Lord together, or pray quietly in tongues, or just relax and chat while the power flowed into Albert's body. At other times the Lord would guide us to minister inner healing alongside the soaking prayer as he revealed to us painful memories from the man's past.

Long after we left the house Albert would frequently sense the effects of the ministry upon his body. Vibrations, or a feeling of warmth, would sometimes wake him in the night as the healing work continued.

One evening, as we approached the house to minister, Freda was waiting for us at the front door, her face all aglow.

'Guess what!' she called jubilantly. 'His toes have turned pink!'

'What do you mean, his toes have turned pink?' I asked.

She smiled. 'I've never seen his toes pink all the years I've known him,' she explained as we followed her into the sitting room. 'His circulation has been so poor that they've always been white.'

As the weeks turned into months, though, we all needed much persistence. Sometimes John and I didn't feel like going to Albert but we still went.

Always the Lord would make it very clear when we were to finish a session. Sometimes it was evident because we knew that the healing flow had stopped. On other occasions one of us might receive a word to show that it was time to close.

The weekly ministry to Albert was to continue for eighteen months. During that period the Lord healed many of his memories and did a deep inner work in his life. And as he experienced this inward healing he was also healed physically.

Eventually he was able to discard the medical corset which he had worn for his back since the war.

A girl who also benefited from soaking prayer lived over an hour's journey away in Sheffield. Shirley, who was in her teens, was blind, and her grandmother, who attended our meetings in another village, had been praying for her for a long time.

The Lord showed me that I was to minister soaking prayer to this girl and I was given a promise which I believed meant that she would be healed.

One day when the Lord's power was upon me I knew that it was to give away to Shirley, so I travelled with her grandmother to Sheffield.

Shirley's parents welcomed us into their lounge. But as soon as I approached the girl herself she went and sat in a corner and started screaming loudly, 'I hate you! I hate God! Leave me alone!'

I discerned the presence of evil spirits, so asked to be left alone with Shirley. Gently but firmly I calmed her down. Then I took the authority of Jesus over the spirits and cast them out. The change in Shirley was dramatic.

After that I travelled regularly to Sheffield and often John came with me. Over a period of time Shirley's personality was marvellously transformed. Often too, during ministry, she could see partially for a while. At other times she had several visions of Jesus and would tell her grandmother, 'Jesus came to me in the night and I could see him clearly.'

But the apparent improvement in Shirley's vision was not maintained and her physical healing did not materialize. Eventually it was diagnosed that her blindness was a result of an incurable condition which affected her whole body.

However, she had come to know Jesus as her Saviour and her mother had joined a church and been confirmed.

Our first experiences of soaking prayer had been demanding but rewarding and we valued what the Lord had taught us. Soaking prayer was to become a method of healing which would play a major part in our ministry.

While we continued to give out we also found it essential to take in. So we began worshipping at another parish church, and in the week we would attend interdenominational charismatic meetings.

One evening we went to a healing service at Rotherham conducted by a Pentecostal evangelist. John was still feeling depressed and went forward to receive the laying on of hands.

'I am seeing a beautiful rose,' the evangelist said as he ministered to John. 'Crowds and crowds are coming to drink in of its fragrance. You will have a big ministry, for crowds of people will come to partake of what you have to share from the Lord.'

As we left the meeting John was looking happier.

'That really uplifted me!' he said enthusiastically. 'I'd begun to lose hope about the Lord using me very much again.'

I put my arm around him. 'Perhaps you'll find he'll use you more because of what you've been through,' I suggested. 'And that was real confirmation, coming from someone who had never met you!'

While all this was going on we heard of a possible opening for John in Singapore. He had done national service on the island twenty years previously and had always wanted to take me there. He wrote to make enquiries but we told nobody.

Then we were approached by three people. One had seen the four of us walking across the sea. Another, while praying, saw an ocean liner with no coastline in sight and the third had an impression of a map of the Far East. In addition, the Lord spoke to us over a period of six months about using us in a far country. We grew very excited about the prospect and had a great longing to go there.

For a while we thought that we really were going to Singapore. But then we learned that there would be difficulty over the boys' education. John also had a mole removed from his back which proved to be malignant and the doctor advised us to remain in this country for five years until John could be pronounced clear of the trouble.

Eventually we were told that the door to Singapore was closed. At first we were shattered but it was amazing how swiftly we lost our strong desire to go there!

We concluded that if it had been the Lord speaking about an overseas ministry for us, then this must lie in the future.

It was by then over a year since John had been taken ill and he was coming out of his silent stage, so we talked and prayed together much more. One day in the study we felt particularly frustrated about everything.

'Lord, we just want to do the right thing,' we prayed. 'We still trust you, and we'll do whatever you want. We don't mind what it is, even if it means no ministry!'

'But we don't understand why all this has happened to us. We feel bruised and battered and we just wonder when it's going to stop. We cannot take much more, Lord...!'

There was a moment's silence and then the Lord spoke through John: 'You will have one more bundle of sadness, then many bundles of gladness.'

So there was more to come. But at least the end of our traumas was in sight.

I I

'One More Bundle of Sadness'

We did have a roof over our heads and we were under no pressure to move. The vicar of a parish in the Church of England is legally secure and under normal circumstances no one can shift him.

But John had been out of action at Merston Mill and Wilfirth churches for over twelve months and they would be needing a new vicar soon. So at the end of the year John voluntarily resigned from being vicar of the two parishes.

We were still unsure where the Lord wanted us to be in the future. But we were both certain by then that in some way we would be continuing the ministry of laying on of hands.

John was having the occasional days when he was ill, but he had made tremendous progress and was gradually easing off taking the tablets.

His improvement was accelerated further by the continual ministry which he was receiving. There were psychological chains to be severed, and much forgiving to be done, and he was able to release to the Lord all who had wronged or hurt him.

He experienced a wonderful new freedom within and the result was a more confident and capable man. I could see him being restored to us not only as he used to be but also with additional strength of character.

It had been a long time since Stephen and Paul, now thirteen and ten, had related much to their father. But

110

recently we had begun to go out more as a family again. Most Saturdays we went to the Huddersfield shops, where the boys would spend their pocket money on records.

One Saturday afternoon early in March we were preparing to go 'to town' as usual. John and I were ready before the boys, so we decided to get the car out and wait in it for them.

Our garage was located in a difficult situation, so we had to back out into a fairly main road and then park opposite the vicarage. From there we had an excellent view of the back entrance, from which the boys would emerge, and of the steps leading down to the driveway.

We watched as the boys left the house and walked towards us. Paul was talking excitedly to Stephen, looking up at him. They were discussing which Elvis Presley records they intended to purchase.

What took place next is what every parent dreads. They reached the road and Stephen stopped at the kerb, but Paul had his eyes on us and ran straight across. Terror gripped me as I saw what was going to happen. I called out frantically, 'Paul, no!' But the oncoming car hit him full in the stomach and hurled him high into the air. He landed about fifty yards along the road. John and I leapt out of the car and raced to the spot.

At first we thought that he was dead but as we knelt beside him he moaned and we realized that he was unconscious. His face was blue and his head had obviously taken a battering. One of his eyes was full of blood and his legs were also bleeding.

I looked at John and blurted out, 'Ambulance!' He jumped up quickly and sprinted back to the vicarage. He tried to keep calm as he spoke the details into the phone. Then he hurried back to me.

Directly he had left me I had spoken quietly another word: 'Jesus'. For in that moment I had been aware of the Lord's lovely presence. He was there, just as he always was: part of our family, present in what we were undergoing.

A crowd gathered and we all waited anxiously for the ambulance to arrive. The lady who had driven the car which had hit Paul was crying. I attempted to comfort her.

'I know it wasn't your fault!' I assured her.

'He seemed to come from nowhere!' she said shakily. 'I thought I'd hit an animal of some sort.'

The ambulance arrived, and then took us at breakneck speed to the hospital six miles distant, its sirens wailing. I felt a horrible sensation in the pit of my stomach, and relived the similar journey ten years previously with my sister Linda. Paul even seemed to look like her lying there.

The driver kept turning his head and asking his partner whether Paul was all right. It suddenly dawned on me that they were not certain whether he would make it to the hospital. I felt sick.

'He could be terribly injured internally,' I thought. 'I've known something was going to happen to him ever since we lived at Wunford. Please don't let him die, Lord!'

I held on to John and Stephen as we swerved dangerously round another bend.

'Be careful!' I called out automatically.

'Don't worry, madam,' said the ambulance man calmly, 'we're police trained.'

When we arrived at the hospital Paul was whisked away from us and we were ushered into a small room and brought the inevitable cup of tea. We gulped it down gratefully, each of us staring into space, silently suffering our own inner agony.

After a while a nurse appeared.

'He's in intensive care,' she said kindly. 'Would you like to see him?'

We nodded and followed her as she led the way to a small, glass-panelled room with just the one bed where Paul lay. He looked much the same, except that now he had three tubes attached to different parts of his body. We looked down at him helplessly. There seemed little that we could do.

'Can I ring you for news?' I asked the nurse anxiously on our way out. 'Even during the night?'

'Aye, of course,' she replied sympathetically, 'and tomorrow you'll be able to speak with doctor.'

On the way home John and I both thought of the same thing: we would ring as many people as possible all over the country who we knew would pray positively for Paul's recovery. We had seen that miracles could be achieved through prayer and a miracle was what we needed then. We were thankful to have so many friends to call upon in a crisis.

I stayed up all night, drinking coffee, praying spasmodically, and ringing the hospital constantly. At one point the night nurse said, 'He's settled down to sleep now.'

I was surprised to learn that people still keep to the natural rhythms of sleeping and waking while in their unconscious state.

During one of my sessions of prayer I had a very vivid picture of Paul in hospital. He was in a large ward and his bed was just inside the door, on the left. He was sitting up laughing and piles of letters were strewn all over his bedclothes. I grasped hold of that picture in the hope that I would see him well again.

The night dragged by and the next morning, Sunday, we hastened to the hospital to hear the doctor's verdict. As we entered his room he smiled at us reassuringly.

'He's still unconscious,' he explained, 'but there's no brain damage and surprisingly, no internal injuries.'

We both heaved a sigh of relief.

'We can never tell with head injuries,' the doctor continued, 'but *if* he comes round there's no reason why he shouldn't eventually return to complete normality.'

Our hearts leapt thankfully.

'That's good news, doctor,' my husband said smiling. 'So we have to wait and see if he comes round now.'

'That's right. But I cannot promise when that might be.'

After leaving the doctor we went straight to intensive care to see Paul. We talked to him naturally, just in case he could hear us. Then we laid our hands on him and prayed for about half an hour, mainly in tongues.

On the way home our conversation was all about Paul and his accident. We drew up at some red traffic lights and suddenly I had the thumps. Almost immediately John said quietly, 'The Lord is saying, "This is the bundle of sadness I told you about."' We stared at each other in astonishment. We had both completely forgotten that the Lord had ever said it! But we found it strangely comforting to be reminded.

Back at the vicarage we also derived much comfort from the prayers and support of our friends, acquaintances and even total strangers in many places. And that evening our suffragan bishop called to say that he too had been to minister to Paul in the hospital.

The next few days and nights dragged interminably. It was impossible to settle down to anything, for all that mattered was that Paul should regain consciousness. We spent most of our time either at the hospital or answering the phone. And Stephen busied himself by compiling a book for his brother.

'It's for him to stick things in when he gets better,' he explained, 'and there are puzzles for him to do.' Stephen was missing Paul, for generally the two of them got on very well together.

Meanwhile, at the hospital, our unconscious son was being subjected to various tests. The doctors seemed so surprised about the absence of internal injuries that a series of different specialists were called in to examine him. But their verdicts were the same.

When we visited Paul we continued to minister soaking prayer to him. We also chatted to him and played his favourite Elvis cassettes, leaving them for the nurses to play to him as well.

On the fourth day I squeezed Paul's hand and said to him softly, 'If you can hear me, darling, try and wiggle your fingers.' We were thrilled when a moment later one of his fingers moved slightly.

On the fifth day he came round. After a while he was dimly aware of a picture on the wall. And later, as we entered the room, we saw that his eyes were wide open. He smiled wanly at us and then, in a croaky voice, asked, 'Have you been to town?'

Overflowing with joy we replied, 'No, not yet, darling!'

Before we left we held his head while the nurse moistened his parched lips with a little drink and encouraged him to take one or two sips.

'What a relief!' I exclaimed as we stepped outside into the corridor. 'We'll be able to sleep easier tonight!'

The next morning when we arrived at the intensive care unit we were pleasantly surprised.

'He's not here any more,' the nurse said triumphantly. 'He's eaten a piece of toast for breakfast and been taken to the children's ward.'

'That's great!' I said jubilantly.

We walked briskly along the lengthy corridors until we found the children's ward, and there he was in the bed opposite the door.

His face lit up when he spotted us. 'What am I doing here, Mum?' he asked.

'You forgot to do your green cross code, darling!' I gave him a big kiss.

'Yes,' said John, grasping his hand firmly, 'you've given us all quite a fright. Never mind, you'll soon be better now.'

Paul thought for a moment, then said, 'Can you get me that Elvis record, "California Holiday", please? I was going to buy it with my pocket money.'

'Yes, of course,' I said soothingly. I was so grateful to have him alive that I would have gladly bought him anything.

As we were leaving I remarked to John, 'They've put him in the wrong bed! *That's* where he should be.' I pointed to the bed just inside the door, on the left. John smiled but said nothing.

After we had gone, the nurse told Paul that he was going to be taken for some tests.

'Come on,' she said, pushing a wheelchair towards him, 'I'll help you in.'

'I don't need that!' he thought indignantly. 'I can walk all right.' He climbed out of bed. But when his feet touched the ground he had a shock. They gave way and the nurse caught him as he fell. Reluctantly he let her help him into the chair.

When he returned to the ward it was teatime.

'Would you like a little ice cream, Paul?' the nurse asked him. 'I'll feed you.'

'Yes, please!' he answered eagerly. But he was puzzled. 'I can feed myself,' he thought. But as he attempted to eat it on his own he discovered that his limbs were uncoordinated and however hard he tried he kept missing his mouth. This was very frustrating, but he persevered, and in the end he succeeded.

After tea he pricked up his ears when he heard that there was an Elvis film on television that evening.

'Fantastic!' he thought. 'My favourite!'

When the film came on he watched enthralled for the first few minutes, but then his eyes became heavy and he was battling to keep them open. He fought hard against it, but very soon he was sound asleep.

The next day when we arrived at the ward there was another child in the bed which our son had occupied, but I knew where to look for Paul!

He was just inside the door, on the left, sitting up in bed laughing, and piles of letters were scattered all over the bedclothes. His headmaster had been to visit him, bringing with him a letter from every child in Paul's class.

What I was observing at that moment was an exact reproduction of the picture which had come into my mind while I was praying for Paul during the night following his accident.

In the next few days he made rapid progress. He was helped to walk again and although his eye was still full of blood he was soon enjoying himself with the other children in the dayroom and chatting away non-stop to the nurses.

He also hungrily devoured several packets of Jaffa cakes which he had asked us to bring him. He had not eaten for days, but he was making up for lost time.

We were overjoyed when we were able to bring him back home after only ten days in hospital and we praised the Lord for restoring him.

One Saturday morning soon afterwards I went out shopping leaving Paul and Stephen playing together. John was in the study, preparing for one of the healing services which we had been asked to take at churches in the area.

While I was gone, the Lord spoke clearly to my husband and when I returned I could sense a very definite change in his attitude towards me. He greeted me at the front door. Then he said, 'I'll unload these groceries for you. You go and sit in the lounge and I'll make you a nice cup of tea. Then I'd like to talk to you.'

Gratefully I flopped on to the settee, kicked off my shoes, and put my feet up.

'This is good,' I thought, settling down, 'I'm going to make the most of this!'

Very soon John joined me and we drank our tea together.

'Come over here,' he said warmly, 'and sit on my lap for a while.' Willingly I did so, glad of the opportunity for an extra cuddle! He put his arms around me gently and looked lovingly into my eyes. Then he spoke softly.

'I want to thank you, darling, for the way you've always stood by me, especially during my illness. I realize now that I've taken you far too much for granted over the years. But I don't want to any more. I want to be a better husband.' He paused. 'I know that in the past I've neglected you and the boys. I've even neglected myself—all for the sake of 'the work'. But the Lord has shown me that my priorities were wrong. *He* comes first, even before his work. And next to him comes my family.' He sighed and I stroked his hair.

'I aim to make a fresh start with the Lord's help,' he said confidently. 'I'm forty at the end of this month and they say life begins at forty.' I grinned while he continued.

'I need a more balanced life, with more exercise and relaxation. I'm going to work at that. I'm also going to try and be a better father to the boys. But most of all I intend to lavish love on you. I want to make you really happy, because I do love you!'

For once I was lost for words, and as he kissed me tenderly my love for him welled up afresh.

Two months later John finished his medication. His healing, which had taken over eighteen months, was complete. Many things had contributed to this: medical and psychiatric help, drugs and the process of time, prayer and ministry, the help and encouragement of his wife and friends and, in the latter stages, the fact that he did much to help himself.

A few days afterwards we were sitting at our favourite spot, by the waterfall, reflecting upon all that had happened.

'You know,' said John thoughtfully, 'when I used to sing those words, "Break me, melt me, mould me, fill me", I had no idea what I was saying really! The words are so easy to sing but so hard to experience.' He looked up at the clear blue sky. 'Do you remember when I ministered at Hainault how I used to say to you, "I just don't know how to pray for people with depression and mental illness"?'

I nodded. 'Yes,' I sighed. 'You'll know how to pray for them now, and you'll be able to identify with such people.' I smiled. 'But I think the people who have to *cope* with the depressed and mentally ill need just as much prayer. *I'll* be able to identify with *them*!'

John turned his gaze to the rushing water and said quietly, 'Three years ago we used to sit here and wonder when the axe was going to strike, or what it would be like in the dark rooms, or in the middle of an earthquake. No way could we have imagined what was to come! But the Lord's been with us and he's brought us through.'

Gratefully we lifted our hearts to him in praise and worship. The sights and sounds of spring were all around us. The wild flowers were blossoming and the birds singing. They spoke of a new beginning and heralded the probability of more encouraging times.

12

'The First Six Months Are the Worst'

The bishop had been negotiating for a council house for us, and we had already been to look over one at Merston but had taken an instant dislike to it. Then another became available.

This one was quite different. A Christian lady had lived in it for over forty years until her death, and the moment that we entered we sensed a peaceful atmosphere. We knew that this was going to be our new home and arranged to move in on the last day of June.

We began to prepare, still uncertain about how we would use our ministries. But as we were packing up a friend who was helping us shared a picture which she had seen while praying: 'There was a huge joint of meat on your doorstep,' she explained, 'and I had the words clearly: "Joint calling"!'

We were extremely amused. The Lord is so often homely and humorous. It was heartening to know that, while John and I would each continue our separate ministries, the Lord was still going to use us jointly as well.

By the time that moving day dawned we had sold or given away much of our furniture. It was only a short distance to Merston, but when we arrived at the council estate we were suddenly in a totally different environment.

Our new home was adjacent to the road at the end of a row of five houses. At the other end lay a vast playing field and recreation ground, and in the distance the lovely Yorkshire moors.

Behind our block was a communal lawn. Children played there, dodging the lines full of washing to retrieve their tennis balls. Neighbours gathered in small groups, laughing and chatting and enjoying the sunshine.

Once inside our house it was strange to see people walking directly past our window and to watch them popping in and out of each other's homes. One woman sat on her doorstep, drinking tea and smoking. The ice cream van with its familiar jingle brought a fresh burst of activity. An elderly man went past licking a cornet, and children scampered to ask for money to buy lollies.

The whole scene was very different from the comparative isolation of the vicarage. Yet very quickly and smoothly we merged into it.

Within days of our moving, our next door neighbour, Heather, was sitting at our kitchen table drinking coffee and pouring out her troubles. After listening and chatting a while we invited her to attend our Friday evening home meeting. This had previously been the parish fellowship but was then called 'Breath'. The Lord had given the title to John and the initials stood for 'Believers Renewed, Evangelizing, Adoring, Testifying, Healing'.

Heather came to the meeting and was overwhelmed by the love which she received there. In a short time she came to accept Jesus as her Saviour and later was baptized in the Holy Spirit.

But one day there was a knock on our back door and we found Heather standing outside in tears.

'It's books,' she said as I led her into the kitchen and put the kettle on. 'None of what happens in those Christian story books happens to me. The people in them do such wonderful things and everything seems to go right for them, but my life is such a struggle.'

I gave her some tissues and put my arm around her.

'We've found life a struggle, too, sometimes,' I said gently, 'even with Jesus to help us. You mustn't expect to model

120

your life on the people in books. God made you *you*.'

'Yes,' agreed John, pouring out the tea. 'The experiences related in these books are meant to encourage you, but if they are having the opposite effect I suggest you give up reading them for a while. Just read the Bible for now, and take things one step at a time.'

'I think I will,' Heather said. 'Perhaps I'm trying to learn too much too quickly.'

She soon informed her friends about us, first one and then another gradually came along to the meeting. They, too, were converted, and as the news spread it appeared to set off a chain reaction.

It was not easy for these new converts. Several discovered that becoming Christians brought fresh problems for them, for they had to rearrange their whole lifestyles!

Another of our neighbours, Rachel, received healing for her hand one night at our meeting. She belonged to the local Baptist chapel situated on the brow of the hill just along the road from us.

Soon afterwards I was invited there to speak to the women's meeting. I shared what Jesus is doing today, and at the close Elsie, the elderly lady leading the meeting, asked me to pray for her.

'It's my legs!' she said wearily. 'I've had them in bandages for fifteen years now. It's an incurable skin disease. They weep all the time.'

I knelt on the floor to pray and laid my hands on her legs. Immediately I closed my eyes I discerned that the disease was caused by an evil spirit. So before praying for healing I rebuked the condition in Jesus' name.

A few days later there was a tap at our door and Rachel stood there, bursting to tell us something.

'Elsie's been healed completely!' she announced. 'She wants you to go and visit her in her home.'

'Praise the Lord!' I exclaimed. 'Where does she live?'

Elsie lived a few doors away from the chapel. So later that evening I made my way there. When she opened the door the old lady could hardly contain herself.

'Look,' she said excitedly, 'my legs! I can actually see my legs! I'm wearing stockings for the first time for fifteen years! I just don't know how to thank you. Do you think you could pray for my neck while you're here, please?'

'I'd be glad to,' I said smiling.

Later I returned home in high spirits. It had been so encouraging to observe Elsie's joy that I felt that I was the one who had been blessed.

Lucy was one of many who came for personal counselling. She arrived early one morning looking very worried.

'I know the Lord reveals things to you both,' she said hesitantly. 'I'm concerned about my eyes, in case there's something seriously wrong. For some time now I've suffered with headaches and double vision. Will you pray for me?'

'Yes, of course,' we replied, helping her to relax in a chair. We began to pray and spent time waiting upon the Lord. After a while I saw vividly the face of a small boy with ginger hair. When I told Lucy she exclaimed, 'That's a boy who used to live next door to us when I was a child. I used to play with him.'

After that I saw a playground and John saw a tree. Lucy was amazed.

'You've been describing the exact spot where I had a serious accident when I were young,' she said. 'I suffered a nasty head injury.'

We continued to pray, and then John said to Lucy, 'I believe there's nothing seriously wrong with your eyes. The root cause of the trouble lies in the past when you had the accident.'

She smiled at us and then stated calmly, 'That's what they told me at hospital, but I just wanted to check that they were right!'

As Lucy was saying goodbye we heard the clippity-clop of horses' hooves outside. This was a regular sound, as riding is a popular pursuit in the area. I looked longingly at the riders as they trotted past.

'I know funds are low, darling,' I said wistfully as I closed the door, 'but for some time now I've had an irresistible urge to take up riding. They say it's cheap to have lessons around here, and it seems an ideal method of relaxing after being with people all the time. At least a horse is not going to start telling us all its problems!'

John laughed. 'Book up some lessons then, if that's what you want to do. I'd like to learn to swim if I can. After that I might even join you, if the Lord provides.'

A few weeks later we were both enjoying our new hobbies. I reflected on how the quality of our lives was already improving. John was becoming a much more thoughtful and attentive husband, and gradually he was building up a better relationship with the boys again. We were becoming more of a family once more, and I felt very relieved. Paul had been baptized in the Holy Spirit before starting secondary school and played the guitar and sang at our meetings. Stephen was preparing to be confirmed.

It was not long before the bishop called to see us. He settled himself comfortably on the sofa and remarked first about the brightness and cosiness of the lounge. It was our only room downstairs apart from the kitchen, but with the purple carpet and red and white wallpaper it looked very striking.

'Well now,' he said officially, 'I expect you wish to specialize.'

We looked at each other.

'Yes, that's what we'd like to do,' John answered.

For thirteen of the fifteen years of our married life we had lived in parochial situations. But we had found it increasingly difficult to limit the sort of ministry which the Lord had given us to parish boundaries. As soon as people heard what we were doing we seemed to break out of them!

But if we chose to do this specialized ministry full time, there was a problem. Apart from a very small sum received each month from the Church Commissioners, it would mean relying on gifts for our income, and the ministry itself would have to be a 'faith ministry'. However, this didn't deter us as we were very sure that it was the Lord who was calling us and it was all in his hands.

After the bishop had gone we hugged one another enthusiastically.

'If we needed any further confirmation of what we're to do that's it!' remarked John.

'Yes,' I agreed happily, 'now the two can meet all the time: our ministry and the people who really want it.'

John nodded. 'This must be what the Lord's been preparing us for,' he added.

A few weeks before Christmas we received some welcome visitors. My sister Rosemary, her husband Ron and their three children were over from Australia, and they had arranged to stay with us for a few days.

We thought that they would like to view some of the local places of interest, so we took them out; but the bitterly cold winds soon drove us back indoors again. Winter in Yorkshire is very different to the climate which they had been used to, and it was much cosier to sit around the fire and talk. We had not seen one another for five years so there was a lot of news to catch up on.

We told them what had happened to us during that period and explained about our ministry. Rose and Ron were finding it difficult to understand what we were planning to do.

Eventually Ron asked, 'Where's the money coming from?'

'That's a good question,' John replied. 'We're hoping it will come in through gifts and through offerings at meetings we take.'

There was a brief silence and they looked a little mystified.

'Perhaps they think we've gone crazy!' I thought. 'Maybe we have!'

Over the Christmas period we sent out our regular newsletter and endeavoured to explain to our friends the fresh step of faith that we had taken. Already we were finding it very hard to manage on such a low income and the doubts were beginning to creep in. But we were encouraged by two letters from Christians who had taken similar steps.

'The first six months are the worst,' wrote someone.

'They certainly are!' we said when we read it.

In the other letter a couple offered some very wise advice

from their own experience: 'Spend the money as it comes in on the next items which you need—the rest will follow.' As time went on we remembered this advice and found it to be invaluable.

Early in the new year a group of people accompanied us to a Trevor Dearing rally near Sheffield. After the meeting John and I were drawn to one side by a Christian lady whom we hardly knew.

'I hope you don't mind my asking,' she said quietly, 'but are you in financial need? I've just been left a small sum of money and I would like to give a tithe to the Lord's work. As I was praying about it I kept having the words, "Chris and John, Chris and John".'

'Thank you, Jesus!' we said gratefully and she promised to send us a cheque.

Before we returned home we were talking with Trevor.

'I've been invited to take more meetings than I can fit in this year,' he remarked. 'Would you like me to suggest you for the ones I can't manage?'

We were delighted. But on the journey home we wondered if anyone would actually want us instead of him! However, when we later prayed about it the Lord said, 'This will be a year of advance. I will develop your ministry. At first it will be like a walk. Then it will increase to a trot, progress to a canter, and eventually you will be galloping!'

Although we were involved with many denominations, John, as an Anglican clergyman, wished to be particularly associated with the Church of England. We had been going to church in Skelmanthorpe, a village the other side of Huddersfield. John Alex, the vicar, was a friend of ours. He was renewed in the Holy Spirit and we had already taken a healing service there. Now my John was appointed Honorary Assistant Minister at the church and began preaching there regularly.

In the meantime we received one or two invitations from outside Yorkshire to take healing missions. We found these very fulfilling.

But although the love offerings given at these were generous they only covered the immediate expenses of the ministry. We still didn't have enough money to provide adequately for a family of four.

One day we actually ran out of food. All that we had in the house was a jar of beetroot.

'You'll be all right,' John quipped, 'but I don't like beetroot!'

I sighed. 'What on earth are we going to do when the children come home from school?' I said worriedly. 'There's nothing to give them for tea. I do think the Lord leaves things rather late sometimes.'

At that moment a surprise visitor arrived, one of the leaders from Merston Mill church. He had recently been ill and he thanked us for our prayers. We talked about what was happening in the area. Then, as he left, he put a ten pound note on the kitchen table.

Directly he had gone I almost ran to the local shops and replenished our empty cupboards with basic foodstuffs.

There were other, similar occasions when we were desperate for provisions and the Lord supplied them in unexpected ways.

One day while I was walking on the moors I found a halfpenny and popped it into my purse. At lunch time that day we planned to have biscuits and cheese, but there was no cheese left and I only possessed 22½ pence.

At the local supermarket I felt embarrassed at asking for a very small piece of cheese and as it was weighed I watched uneasily in case I wouldn't have sufficient to pay for it.

'That piece is 22½ pence,' the shop assistant declared matter of factly. I breathed a sigh of thankfulness for the extra halfpenny!

Not far from where we lived is a reservoir. It is situated in a beautiful spot, with tall majestic pine trees towering above it and a well worn winding pathway circling around it.

During the winter the terrain was rough. But John and I loved to walk there, so we donned our boots, wrapped up well and trudged along the path.

'I don't know how we're going to pay that gas bill,' I said

to John as he took my hand, 'let alone the car and the phone.'

He attempted to reassure me. 'Well, we've managed so far, with the Lord's help.'

'But it's humiliating,' I protested, 'having to depend so much upon other people. And it's unsettling when we never know quite how much money we're going to have.'

John helped me over a stile. 'If you're feeling less sure about what we're doing,' he said, 'we'd better ask the Lord to confirm it through someone else. The frustrating thing is that we can't share about financial problems with many people.'

'Esther would understand,' I said, 'we could ask her to pray about it.' Esther was a prophetess who was used much in speaking direct words from God. She belonged to the Breath Fellowship and was a member of a local Elim church.

The next evening we called at her house and confidentially told her what was on our minds. Before we left we prayed together and Esther had a lengthy prophecy:

'I have called you and chosen you,' saith the Lord, 'and I am testing you for a reason: that you might prove your faithfulness to me. For many are called but give up when the going becomes tough.

'When I walked the earth I was tested and tried. I had nowhere to lay my head and often I did not know where things were coming from. I will always provide for you and will speak to people about you. Continue to trust me fully.

'Do not I live with you? Do not I commune with you as you go about your house and lie upon your bed? I see the things that are going through your minds, and I care. For your ministry is my ministry, and, as you go, so people will know that I have sent you.'

In the following years we would be faced with much financial hardship, but the Lord's words through Esther remained a source of encouragement to us.

Occasionally John was eligible to apply for a grant from the Church of England. At one point we had a massive car repair bill which we were unable to pay, and John asked for assistance. He had to give an account of all our finances to a church officer. Then we waited hopefully for the outcome.

One morning, in response to this request, a cheque arrived in the post for about £400.

We were overjoyed—until we read the letter enclosed with it. The grant had been made on condition that we sold our car. Since half our income was being spent on this it was felt that we should be able to manage more easily without it.

'Oh no!' I gasped. 'How can we do a travelling ministry without a car?'

'I don't know,' John answered glumly, staring first at the cheque, then at the letter. 'But we desperately need this money!'

Over the next ten days we tussled with the problem of what to do. We looked at it from every angle but could see no alternative but to keep the car, and, when we prayed, the Lord said, '*I* will show you when to sell your vehicle.'

Reluctantly we came to the conclusion that the only course to take was to return the cheque. John wrote that we were very grateful for the offer but regretted that we were unable to fulfil the conditions required.

Four days later the church officer called on us. We explained the circumstances more fully and the consequence was that we were granted half the amount unconditionally.

Meanwhile, we were faced with a continuing problem of another sort. Like thousands of other women in the north I was fearful of going out anywhere alone after dark or in lonely places.

There was a murderer at large, known as the Yorkshire Ripper. He had already brutally killed a number of women, one of them in Huddersfield, yet the police seemed unable to track him down. It was likely that a woman was shielding him. There was constant speculation about the case: in the shops, in the launderettes, in the restaurants and on the local radio.

One evening the four of us had travelled to a meeting at York, and we arrived back home in the early hours of the morning.

It was when we went upstairs to bed that we noticed. High above the landing was a trapdoor which led into the loft. This was always kept firmly shut but now it was wide open.

A shiver went through my spine.

'Do you think there's someone up there?' I whispered.

13

'Turn Again, Whittington!'

John peered up into the darkness.

'It's not very likely,' he murmured. But I didn't think that he sounded too confident. We all listened intently for a moment but could hear nothing.

'It's an extremely windy night,' John remarked. 'Perhaps the wind shifted the door. I'm sure there's a simple explanation. If only we had a ladder long enough I could investigate for you.'

As I undressed and climbed into bed I felt a little nervous and once in bed my imagination ran riot. At two o'clock I decided that I had to know whether there was anyone up there or not.

'You'll have to call the police, darling,' I declared.

An hour later two burly policemen arrived.

'You'll think I'm silly,' I said sheepishly.

'Not at all, madam,' they replied, 'we're being called out all the time. We've even had to escort women from their houses to their garages. No one can take any chances.

In a short time a thorough search was made of the whole loft area and we were reassured that there was no one there. I breathed a sigh of relief. But the mystery remained: how did the door come to be open?

It was to be another year before the Ripper was finally caught and later sentenced to life imprisonment. Then once again women could walk the streets without fear.

Meanwhile, we noticed that several of the prophecies which had been given to us two and a half years previously were coming to pass one after another. A significant one concerned two of the shops in Merston.

The Lord had told us, 'You will be ministering to the people in these shops.' When he had said it it had seemed to us very unlikely. But there was a lady that I had felt compelled to pray for who used to walk past the vicarage occasionally. I didn't know her, but felt a strong drawing towards her and remarked to John that she was in great need. I prayed for her regularly, and later she opened a shop in the village. In order to develop a relationship with her I started going into the shop and I discovered that her name was Joy.

While this was going on, Pauline, still carrying around her unwanted prescription, was constantly witnessing about Jesus. We would sometimes see her in the street praying with people. She was a regular customer at another shop in the village and invited the lady who owned it to our Breath meeting.

Nancy accepted the invitation and over a period of time received some deep ministry and counselling. One evening she brought Joy with her to the meeting and I was able to share with Joy how I had prayed for her for so long.

A few months afterwards, when Joy was in hospital making a remarkable recovery from a mastectomy, we visited her and she said, 'It was you who first brought me to Jesus. I'll always be grateful.'

When Joy was well and back at work she and Nancy held prayer meetings in the shops during the lunch hour and studied the Bible together.

They also brought a number of people along to our monthly healing service at Skelmanthorpe. In particular there was a girl who had been in hospital about her nose, which was blocked. She was unable to sleep at night and the condition appeared to be incurable. But after the service she found that she was healed and this in turn made an impact upon her family.

We were learning, though, that the Lord works in seasons.

Just as in the physical world there are times of sowing and reaping, so it is in the spiritual realm.

There were times, perhaps lasting for several months, when everyone we touched was blessed in an obvious way. But during other periods there was no immediate outward sign of what the Lord was doing.

We had seasons of provision when the money seemed to flow in—just enough to cover our needs. Then it would cease and we wondered when we would be able to pay our bills.

There were seasons of attack. Sometimes the Lord warned us of these before they arrived and he instructed us to stand firm.

There were times of feasting and periods of fasting, times when our guidance was clearcut and others when we walked in the dark.

But in everything that happened we were aware that the Lord had set us on a definite course. One of the things that he said to us was: 'The die is cast. Your ministry will develop, widen and change. One ministry follows another and another follows that. Your present ministry is a training ground. The one that follows will be similar but not the same. During the third I will take you to the ends of the earth.'

Another favourite place where the Lord chose to speak to us was in bed, usually just as we were dropping off to sleep! One night I saw a picture of Dick Whittington with his little bag slung over his shoulder. I thought that it was a ridiculous picture to see, but as it would not go away I shared it with John.

'Whatever does it mean?' I asked him.

John had no hesitation at all.

'It means we're going back down London way,' he answered, and quoted from the old rhyme: 'Turn again, Whittington...Lord Mayor of London.' Then he added, 'That could mean anywhere in the south, I suppose.'

'Thank goodness!' I exclaimed. 'I wonder when?'

John's eyes were closed. 'I'm having an impression of snow,' he said slowly, 'and the Lord is saying, "One more summer and one more winter and after that I will move you.'''

After a moment I said thoughtfully, 'That will take us to spring or summer of next year. That's when Stephen leaves school, so it would be a sensible time to move in any case.'

During the next few days we asked friends to pray about a possible move. One of them was given the word 'Sussex'. We decided to store these things in our minds. If they were from the Lord then they would come to fruition.

More invitations were beginning to come in to take healing missions in different parts of the country. The main purpose of the meetings was to encourage people. They usually consisted of lively worship, ministry of the word, and laying on of hands, but we quickly came to recognize that anything could happen in them!

Before we went on one mission John asked the Lord for the supernatural gift of the word of knowledge in public. He had often used this in personal counselling but knew that it could also be of tremendous value in the meetings. It was not surprising that he soon found himself in a position where he had to use it.

It was the last evening of the mission and everyone thought that the service had finished. It had lasted three hours and there had been queues for the laying on of hands. Suddenly I had a strong anointing upon me. My breath was being taken away and I began to gasp, while my hands were shaking violently. I realized that it was the Lord's power and that he was wishing to say something but I hadn't a clue what it was. John was standing with me at the front of the church and I could feel people staring at me. I bowed my head and silently cried, 'What is it, Lord? What do you want me to do?'

Then I heard John's calm voice beside me speaking gently but with authority: 'The Lord is showing me that there's a lady here who's deeply hurt inside. She needs ministry but she hasn't come forward to receive it, and he wants my wife to lay hands on her.'

You could have heard a pin drop. Then an elderly lady walked unsteadily forward, the tears rolling down her cheeks.

'It's me!' she whispered. 'I know it's me!'

I felt the Lord's compassion for her. 'Isn't it wonderful?' I said to her. 'The Lord wouldn't allow us to go home until he had personally ministered to you!'

I placed my hands on her head and was led to pray a very soothing prayer asking Jesus to heal the deep hurts within her.

After the meeting we were told, 'If anyone needed ministry for deep hurts it was that lady! A few weeks ago her husband committed suicide. He walked up to the garden shed and took some weedkiller.'

Sometimes at missions the minister and his wife are the ones who most require help and encouragement. On one occasion we were staying at a manse, and, unknown to us, Helen, the minister's wife, had been waiting for an opportunity to speak to me alone. On the last day, a Sunday, we had just finished breakfast and everyone else was leaving the table when I felt a nudge to stay.

'Would you like another piece of toast?' Helen asked.

I didn't really want it but I said that I would and while I was eating it she poured out her heart to me. After a while she revealed the root cause of her problems.

'We were rejected by our last church,' she explained shyly, 'and I still feel very hurt inside. I want to go towards the members of this church here but I'm unable to. I suppose it's because I'm afraid of getting hurt and rejected again.'

I immediately identified with how she felt and I prayed with her and ministered to her. I also suggested that she come forward for the laying on of hands at the morning service. She did, together with her husband, and the whole church prayed with us for them.

At the evening service Helen shared with the congregation how she had been feeling towards them. 'But the Lord touched me this morning,' she testified, 'and he set me free.'

Afterwards there was much joy when several church members approached her and warmly embraced her and she was able to respond in a way she had never done before.

It is not always obvious when people have deep hurts.

Many of us put on masks that disguise our inner feelings. They become a form of protection, rather like a shell. The Lord said at one of our meetings, 'I am in the business of gently cracking eggs. The outside shell needs to be cracked so that I may reach through to the deepest needs.'

Tom was a bit like that. He met us at the church door with a beaming smile and gave us our hymn books. The impression gained was of somebody who was extremely happy. But during the service Tom came up for ministry and explained about his deep sorrow.

'I used to work as an evangelist many years ago,' he told me, 'but my twelve year old daughter was killed in an accident and I came right away from the Lord. I want to come back to him tonight. Will you pray that he will equip me to work as an evangelist again?'

I did, and the Lord's power descended mightily upon him as he fell to the floor. During the remainder of the service he stayed there shaking, and uttering terrible heart-rending sobs. But when he was eventually helped up he was radiant.

'I feel like a changed man!' he exlaimed.

When we were invited to a Pentecostal church to take a mission John remarked to me, 'I don't think I'll wear my clerical collar this time. It's very informal.'

'I've an idea that you should,' I said.

He shrugged. 'Oh, all right then!'

We were unaware of the important part John's collar was to play in a whole sequence of events planned by the Lord!

Sonia was a doctor's wife and she noticed the announcement about our healing mission in her local newspaper. She didn't even know where the Pentecostal church was. But she made enquiries, and when she arrived at the first meeting she was pleased to be offered a seat next to somebody that she knew.

As the rally progressed, all sorts of things happened that Sonia was not used to. The singing was loud and enthusiastic and there was also singing in tongues. At several points during the meeting a gift of tongues was manifested, followed shortly afterwards by an interpretation in English. There were prophecies, as well. Most significant of all was the very powerful atmosphere, and she was amazed to witness people overcome while being prayed for. At times she felt like running out. But one thing stopped her: the fact that in the middle of it all was a very respectable Church of England clergyman with a dog collar on!

The next day she rang the pastor's house where we were staying and asked to speak to John. She had so many questions that we arranged to visit her in her home the following morning.

When we arrived, Sonia said brightly, 'As I told my husband what happened at that meeting he sank lower and lower into his chair! We're both Christians, but we've never encountered anything like this firsthand before.'

We talked for several hours and then she asked if we would pray for her to be baptized in the Spirit. We all knelt together by the sofa and the Lord's power descended upon us. During this time I saw a picture of ripples on a pond circling outwards as far as the eye could see. I shared it with Sonia: 'The Lord is saying that the ripples made from what has happened to you will spread far and wide.'

That night she brought her husband Barry to the meeting. At the beginning John asked if anyone would like to share what the Lord had done for them during the mission. Sonia immediately shot to the front, eager to testify about all that had happened. Later her husband, too, was renewed in the Spirit.

Sonia and Barry longed to launch out in using spiritual gifts but didn't know where to begin. There were many practical questions that they wanted to ask. They also knew of many other Christians who were in a similar position and were concerned for them.

So they asked if we could help them all. They wanted teaching, but also training in how and when to use the gifts.

'We'll open up our home for a meeting,' they said, 'and perhaps you can come and show us what to do and help us actually to do it!'

When the time arrived, over thirty people gathered in the

lounge of the doctor's house. Sonia and Barry's minister and other leaders were among them. John taught them from the Bible and our own experience, then encouraged them to launch out in the gifts and in laying on of hands by ministering to one another.

The evening was a blessing to all and was soon followed by a similar one. Many had taken a step further in their walk with the Lord, and Sonia and Barry found a new ministry opening up for them. A regular meeting started in their house and they are still being used very much by the Lord.

Back at home, one of the things that the Lord often said to us was, 'Be ready for anything!'

One day a freelance journalist rang up from Fleet Street, London, and John answered the phone.

'I hear you do exorcisms,' said the reporter, who gave his name as Vincent. 'I'm intending to submit a series of articles on the subject to some periodicals and I'm researching it.'

'Well,' John said guardedly, 'our main ministry is healing. We do some deliverance as part of that, but only very occasionally do we exorcize anyone.'

'All the same,' persisted Vincent, 'I would be interested to hear of your experiences. May I travel up to see you so that we can talk together?'

John agreed and they decided on a date.

'I'll be there about two,' Vincent promised.

When the day arrived, the morning was already booked to minister to Sally. She was a former student at Bible college, now married with two children. Her problems lay in her past and she had asked for inner healing. But as the ministry progressed the room grew icy cold and we were very aware of the presence of evil.

We had noticed on other occasions that demons only tend to manifest themselves among Christians when the power of the Lord is fully released, just as they cried out in the real presence of Jesus when he walked the earth—though they didn't automatically flee at his presence, but had to be told to go.

As we continued to pray and praise, Sally quite suddenly

leapt out of her chair and started slithering around on the floor like a snake, her face contorted. She came leering at us with loud hissing noises. We had no option but to launch into an exorcism.

We came against the evil forces with the authority of Christ. Immediately the hissing stopped and Sally's appearance changed to that of a serpent trying to charm. She half rose from her horizontal position on the carpet and stretched out vertically. Her arms were high in the air, her body twisting and turning, and her face took on an alluring, bewitching expression. During the battle that followed, she alternated between these two manifestations and when the spirit left her she dropped to the floor like a stone and lay as though dead.

After a while she opened her eyes and said, 'Someone at Bible school discerned that I had evil spirits. I was ministered to there, but I thought I was cleared. You see, when I was about ten I started to train to be a medium.'

'Well, let's praise the Lord for what he's done,' John suggested. But no sooner had we started to sing than Sally was taken over again. This time her face was transformed into that of a pig. We encouraged her to cooperate with us when she was able and together we wrestled against principalities and powers.

'I know how that one got there,' Sally remarked afterwards, 'we used to call on the spirit of the pig. Thank God, Jesus has set me free!'

We were all thoroughly exhausted but elated.

'What a pity,' I joked, 'the journalist has missed all the action!' We then explained to Sally about Vincent's appointment.

'Well, you tell him all about me,' she urged on her way out, 'and what the Lord has done today.'

An hour later Vincent arrived.

'If you'd come this morning,' we said to him, 'you would have had a firsthand demonstration. But unfortunately these events cannot always be arranged!'

He switched on his mini cassette recorder, and there was

no stopping us as we graphically described what had happened.

After he had gone I turned to John with a twinkle in my eye.

'Surely it was no coincidence that we had such an up to date story to tell him!' I said.

The telephone continued to ring intermittently with requests for ministry. A woman called Mary asked John if he could visit her elderly mother, who was seriously ill in hospital. He went twice, and she improved slightly after the laying on of hands.

But one morning a letter arrived from Mary.

'My mother has died,' she had written. 'My sister and I believe she should be raised from the dead. Can you help?'

14

'Send 'Em In, Lord!'

John passed the letter to me across the breakfast table.

'Well, how old was this woman?' I asked curiously.

'Eighty-eight,' he answered quietly.

'Gracious!' I exclaimed.

John had the delicate task of explaining over the phone to Mary that her mother, who was a Christian, was best left with the Lord.

'Jesus only occasionally raised the dead,' he reminded her, 'and the examples recorded are of people who died at a much younger age.'

But the incident made us think. The disciples of Christ were commanded to raise the dead as well as heal the sick. Would we ever be ready to do this if the Lord showed us that it was right?

We didn't have much time to pursue the matter, for life was becoming hectic again. The Lord had said not long before, 'You will have your fingers in many pies,' and we had become involved in numerous activities.

Occasionally when we travelled we wondered whether we were in the right place at the right time.

An evangelist in a northern town was extremely keen for us to minister at a healing crusade in a football stadium and when he said that the Christians concerned felt sure that we were the ones to take the crusade meetings we agreed to do this.

140

Soon afterwards he assured us that extensive plans were under way and that the crusade would be supported by many churches and ministers from a very large area. He also said that weekly prayer meetings were being held as part of the preparation and he invited us to take a preliminary mission in the town. John spent a whole week preparing six talks which would help the Christians involved to evangelize, using healing as the point of contact.

But when we arrived we were surprised to find that the mission was in a tiny church and that only about a dozen people had turned up for the first meeting.

The church secretary, a short, stocky man called Bert, led the choruses and he interspersed these with little homilies. The pastor, a tall, thin man called Cecil, played the piano, and he interrupted Bert at various points. John came and sat next to me in the front row of the congregation.

'Where are all the people who are supposed to be supporting the crusade?' I whispered. He shrugged his shoulders.

As the meeting progressed there was a time of open prayer.

'Send 'em in, Lord! Send the sinners in!' one man prayed. Others followed with lengthy prayers expressing the same sentiments. John and I exchanged questioning glances and he whispered, 'I don't think I'll be able to give the talk I've prepared. They're obviously not ready for it.'

When eventually the meeting was handed over to him he gently reminded the congregation that sometimes the Lord wants us to help answer our own prayers.

'People are most likely to come along if we offer to bring them,' he added encouragingly.

After the service, Bert took up this point with us.

'I've always wanted to witness to unbelievers about Jesus,' he said sadly.

My heart sank. If people like this church secretary had no experience of evangelism, how did they expect to fill the football ground?

'We'll pray that you'll get an opportunity to witness,' said John, 'and that the Lord will give you the words.'

In bed that night John and I lay awake for hours discussing the situation. We both felt very disturbed.

'I'm beginning to wonder whether we should have come here,' John said with dismay.

'Surely they could have made a greater effort,' I remarked gloomily, 'all they seem to have done is put up a few posters!'

'I wonder where all the ministers have got to who are supporting the crusade?' John said, staring at the ceiling.

'Well, I feel like going home in the morning!' I exclaimed. 'There seems to be very little that we can do here.'

'We'll have to stay at least for the meetings tomorrow,' John said, 'but if there's no improvement by the evening it may be right to leave Bert and Cecil to take the other services themselves.'

When at last we managed to get off to sleep we both had nightmares.

The next morning Bert was in the town's shopping centre, a huge complex thronged with Saturday shoppers. Wanting to sit down, he saw that the seats provided were filled with people, but he managed to find one space among them.

After a moment he was startled by the voice of the man sitting next to him: 'You're a Christian, aren't you? I'm a Satanist!'

Bert was taken aback. He had never met the man before.

But when he had regained his composure he spent over an hour talking to the man about Jesus and his atoning blood. He found that the words just flowed. God was answering our prayer for him more quickly than he could have imagined! In the end he took the man for pie and peas, a traditional northern dish.

By the time that he arrived at the meeting that afternoon Bert was bursting with excitement and he told the congregation what had happened.

At this meeting John gave a teach-in on guidance. In the front row sat a very large woman in her fifties called Emma. She was obviously not a member of the church and she had arrived late.

While John was speaking she began to comment in low

tones on what he was saying. As he was describing an instance of how the Lord had guided us, Emma called out: 'But it doesn't always work!'

Her interruptions kept disturbing John's train of thought, and I was a little annoyed. Eventually he stopped speaking and patiently explained to her that there would be opportunity for questions afterwards.

During the question session Emma described some of her many problems.

'Can you come and visit me?' she asked. 'I do need help.'

'We'll be there Monday morning,' we promised.

There was a tea provided in the church before the evening rally. This was our first real opportunity to discuss the proposed crusade with the people, but to our surprise the subject was avoided and the conversation was superficial.

Suddenly I felt that I couldn't bear it in there any longer. I got up and walked out of the building.

Once outside in the street I started running.

'Everything about this weekend has been so different from what we expected! I thought. I ran and ran, the tears smarting in my eyes.

'Why are we here, Lord?' I cried aloud in my frustration. 'I don't want to be part of this!'

Then as I passed the bus station I heard the words very clearly: 'Go back!'

It was the still, small voice.

I stopped running, turned around and walked back towards the church. When I opened the door the soloist at the previous meeting was standing there.

'I've been looking for you,' she said. 'Can I see you a moment?'

John joined us and we went through to the vestry. There we ministered inner healing to her and later she testified that her back had also been healed in the process.

We were warned to watch out for Charlie, a little, wiry man with an accordion, who tended to turn up at the church on special occasions.

'If you give him him an inch he'll take a yard,' we were

told. His prayers in church have been known to last for three quarters of an hour!'

Just before the evening service Charlie approached us.

'Can I play my accordion tonight?' he asked.

'Do you mean to accompany the singing?' John said cautiously.

'Oh no,' he replied, 'I mean do a turn, and say a few words. Can I give my testimony?'

John and I exchanged meaningful glances and it was I who answered: 'I don't think there'll be time. Besides, a group of people are travelling here tonight especially to hear my husband. Perhaps you'll get another opportunity,' I added.

There were more people at the service that evening and early on I had some words impressed upon me: 'My light will pierce this darkness.' At the same time John was seeing a picture of nutcrackers and as the meeting progressed we sensed a real breakthrough.

But suddenly Charlie started to pray aloud. He went on and on and on, and people began to fidget. I looked across at John on the platform and met his gaze. Then simultaneously, but very softly to start with, he and I began to sing. In a matter of seconds others joined in and very soon the whole congregation was drowning Charlie's prayer!

During the laying on of hands a woman asked John to pray for a new kidney for her sister. It so happened that John had recently watched a television programme about kidney donors. Apparently there were many of these in the country but because of a lack of communication the kidneys were not always made available in time. So John prayed that a kidney would become available for this woman's sister.

The next day the woman came up to me and said indignantly, 'When I asked your husband to pray for a new kidney for my sister I didn't mean a transplant—that's second-hand! I meant a *new* one. God can do it!'

'Of course he can!' I said. 'But he doesn't only use supernatural methods to answer our prayers. In fact, much of the time he uses natural means. The important thing is that we don't limit God to any one way of working.'

But she remained unconvinced.

At the meeting that afternoon John was in the middle of a teach-in on the gifts of the Spirit when an alcoholic stumbled in. He sat right at the back, and rolled around for a while, but then he sobered up and listened intently to what John was saying. When the time came for the laying on of hands the man came forward. As he was prayed for he was overcome quite suddenly with conviction about his sins, so much so that he cried out aloud, 'Forgive me, Lord! I know I'm a sinner!'

We took him into the vestry and led him to accept Jesus as his own Saviour. But after this he became worried about his drinking problem.

'I wonder if I'll be able to keep up being a Christian,' he said doubtfully.

'You don't have to,' John assured him. 'It won't always be easy but now you have Jesus to give you his strength and power.'

Bert was standing nearby in tears.

'I'll help him, too,' he said. 'He's my brother and I've been praying for him for years to come to the Lord.'

The last day of the mission was a Monday and in the morning, as already planned, we set off to visit Emma. She welcomed us into her spacious lounge and immediately proceeded to share her troubles.

'I'm in such a mess!' she confessed helplessly. 'I've family problems and business worries. I used to be addicted to alcohol, and then to food. The doctor put me on slimming pills but I became addicted to them too.'

She stopped as she noticed me looking at a large picture of Jesus on the wall.

'Yes,' she said hastily, 'I go to mass on Sundays and I see a faith healer during the week. I say my prayers, too, but God seems so far away.'

'That's understandable,' I said gently, 'but in fact he's very near you—only on the outside. And you need him to help you from the inside.'

'What do you mean?' she enquired.

We opened our Bibles and explained to Emma what it means to be a true Christian. For about two hours we talked with her and she asked questions. Then we invited her to pray with us and we all knelt in the middle of the room.

All at once Emma was overcome with sorrow for the life that she had lived and she started sobbing.

'I do want God on the inside!' she cried out desperately. So quite simply John led her in a prayer of commitment, which she repeated with sincerity. Emma still needed to work through her problems, but she was a changed woman, and the next time we saw her she was radiant.

On the previous evening pastor Cecil had told the congregation, 'I feel fettered. Many of you know why.'

In the past he had been mightily used as a prophet, but since a previous church had asked him to leave, he had been so hurt that he felt unable to manifest the gift. However, the Lord had been working in his life, too, for at the last service of the mission he spoke out a powerful prophecy.

As we drove home I exclaimed, 'What an eventful weekend! The Lord obviously had his own ideas of what he wanted to do.'

'Yes,' agreed John, 'and he did "send 'em in" after all!' We both laughed. 'I still don't think they're ready for a big crusade, though,' he went on. 'I'm going to ask to meet the ministers, to see what support there really is.'

In fact the support turned out to be negligible, so we wrote to say that we thought it inadvisable to hold a crusade of that nature that year.

During the autumn I sometimes helped to look after some horses, and my reward for this was free rides. John had by then taken up riding as well, and we both found the hacks through the lovely Yorkshire countryside relaxing and exhilarating. They helped to recharge us after particularly busy periods. At Christmas we enjoyed taking part with other riders in an open air service of carols on horseback.

Stephen, then in his last year at school, was gifted at

writing short stories and drawing profiles. Paul had become very keen on Cliff Richard. Both boys loved to play snooker, and Alex 'Hurricane' Higgins was their champion. champion.

One Sunday afternoon Stephen came bursting into the house.

'Mum! Mum! You remember what happened to Paul? It's happened to Andrew. He's been knocked down by a motor bike. Can you get to the hospital quickly and pray for him?'

Andrew was one of Stephen's friends and he lived just along the road from us. He was a frequent visitor at our house and we called him the good-looking one. We would often catch sight of him doing his paper round on the estate.

The accident had happened in the early hours of Saturday morning when he was walking home from a disco with some friends. He had fractured his skull and had been taken unconscious to a hospital in Wakefield.

On hearing the news John and I decided to go straight to the hospital. Upon our arrival at the neurological unit the nurse would only admit John, because he was a clergyman. She handed him a gown to put on and he went through to where Andrew lay. Several tubes were attached to his body and he was connected to a life-support machine. He felt cold and lifeless when John placed his hands on him.

It was difficult to imagine Andrew as we had known him, so full of life, but that was how John tried to picture him. We had often found it helpful to visualize sick people as healthy while praying for them. For half an hour he prayed in tongues as he kept his hands on Andrew's body.

Meanwhile, I sat outside in the corridor looking out for Andrew's parents. I didn't know them but when they arrived looking anxious and worried I guessed who they were.

'I'm Stephen's mother,' I explained. 'My husband's in there praying for Andrew. We've been through all this with our Paul, and God answered our prayers for him.' Andrew's mother, Carol, collapsed in my arms in tears and I cried with her.

The next day several attempts were made to disconnect

Andrew from the life-support machine, but without success. All day long I found myself praying in tongues for him— while I was doing the housework, the washing, the shopping, all the time. I couldn't get him off my mind.

In the evening John and I went round to his house to see how he was, but there was still no improvement. We were introduced to Carol's parents and were soon sharing more about how Paul had been restored to us. Without knowing quite why, I also found myself describing in detail how Jesus had become real to me. They all listened with rapt attention.

The following day Andrew's condition stabilized, and the day after that he was successfully taken off the life-support machine and regained consciousness. From then on he made rapid progress, and within three weeks he was out doing his paper round.

His parents came to Breath, and Carol told me, 'I didn't believe before, but I do now!'

We learned from Andrew's father that the doctors had not expected his son to live.

'I hope that some day what's happened can be put into print,' he said.

A fortnight later, early in the morning, we were awakened by a banging at our back door. I opened it and was surprised to see Carol standing there, looking very distressed. Immediately I wondered whether Andrew had suffered a relapse, but she said, 'It's my father. Both his kidneys have collapsed and he's been rushed to hospital. He's been asking for John.'

My heart went out to her and I assured her that John would go straight away.

When he arrived at the hospital he found Carol's father in a critical condition, unable to speak. Although John ministered to the man's body he felt led to pray primarily for salvation. Briefly and simply he explained to Carol's father how he could be sure of eternal life and said aloud a prayer of acceptance. The man was able to respond by making signs and noises and John came away feeling satisfied that he was saved.

The next day Carol's father died and the following week

John took the funeral. As we left I remarked to him, 'I can see now why I felt compelled to share so much about Jesus that night when Carol's parents were there. Isn't it great that her father came to know him before he died?'

Gerald had a similar experience. He was a married man in his fifties living in Halifax. At one time he had been on Lord Mountbatten's staff in India. He had also led a very active outdoor life and was fond of rock climbing. But he was suddenly struck down by motor neurone disease, a degenerative condition of the spinal cord which in time affects all the muscles of the body.

Gerald was desperate and asked us to minister to him. We had a number of stimulating discussions in his home and gradually he came to put his trust in the Lord. On each occasion we ministered soaking prayer but after a few sessions there was no sign of any physical improvement and he was confined to a wheelchair.

'Do you still want us to come?' we asked him.

'If you can, please,' he replied, 'the sessions are of such benefit to me spiritually.'

When Gerald later died the Lord impressed on me the words of Mark 9:45: 'It is better for you to enter life lame than with two feet to be thrown into hell.'

Gerald had exchanged his physical disability for a place in heaven.

Ernest was already sure of a place in heaven, but he lost this assurance after he committed a criminal offence. He was known to us because of his lay-preaching and door-to-door evangelism and we had visited him in hospital after he had suffered an apparent heart attack. But we were unaware then that he was already in police custody.

We were therefore surprised to receive a phone call from a prison chaplain informing us that Ernest was on remand in the prison and was asking for us.

The prison was an old grey fortress set on a hill. Huge and foreboding, it dominated the surrounding landscape.

John, with his collar on, went through the security check fairly swiftly. He was able to see Ernest in the quietness of the chaplain's room and there he attempted to comfort a guilt-ridden and repentant man with the assurance that God had truly forgiven him.

The men on remand awaiting trial were treated much the same as those who had already been pronounced guilty and this itself seemed punishment enough for Ernest. But the chaplain was grim-faced as he spoke to John privately after the interview.

'A severe sentence is very likely,' he warned. 'Ernest can expect to go to prison for several years.'

The outlook for him seemed bleak.

15

'Do You Do Healing Too?'

Meanwhile, I was directed to a small, shabby-looking hut where I joined a long queue of other people who were waiting to visit inmates. There were several women there with young babies in their arms and the atmosphere was noisy and smoky.

After giving the names of the men whom we were visiting, we were led across to the main prison building and there we waited for each name to be called out. The warders then ushered us into a room where the inmates were sitting in a long row, very close together.

I immediately spotted Ernest, and went to sit opposite him. There was so much noise that we had to shout to hear one another, and because of the lack of privacy we were unable to talk at a very deep level. When I came away I felt quite discouraged and I felt even worse when I learned from John what the chaplain had told him.

But we were all in for a surprise. Instead of being given a prison sentence, Ernest was committed to a psychiatric hospital. In a short time he was also released from there and reunited with his family.

During the autumn after my picture of Dick Whittington the Lord started speaking to us again about our move.

'A word will be whispered in someone's ear,' he said, 'and that will be passed on. The result will be that I shall bring you to the place I've promised you. Before the last leaf has dropped from the trees, things will have developed with regard to your move.'

We knew that we would have to play our part, so we advertised in the church papers for a house to rent in the south from the following summer.

Then I began to have an impression of a very large building, set in extensive grounds. I saw this several times as the weeks went by.

'I hope it's not where we're going to live,' I said to John, 'because it's *very* large!'

We eventually received seven replies to our advertisement, and we were particularly drawn to one of them which gave details about a house at Southwater, a village near Horsham in West Sussex.

Sarah, the landlord's wife, taught at a girls' school. One day another teacher happened to pass a copy of the *Church Times* to her. It was the one with our advertisement in. Sarah was attracted by the description of our ministry and she cut out our address and popped it into her purse. There it remained for several weeks until she remembered it and showed it to her husband Timothy. It was after Christmas when he wrote inviting us to look over the house.

The day before we were due to go was a Friday and we shared about it at the Breath meeting. The fellowship prayed that the Lord would guide us and Esther had a prophecy: 'I am opening a door for you. I will go with you and there is one you will minister to. There is a reason for this, and it will become apparent.'

We wondered what the reason could be. We were only going to look over a house and had not been expecting to minister to anybody!

The next day our family piled into the car for the two hundred and fifty mile journey to Horsham. Timothy and Sarah lived at Christ's Hospital school, where Timothy was a teacher and we had arranged to stay overnight with them. We found the massive gates at the entrance to the school grounds and drove in. It was some time before we caught sight of the first boarding house, but when we did I could hardly contain my excitement.

'Look!' I exclaimed. 'That's the building I've been seeing!'

Timothy and Sarah welcomed us warmly and we instantly liked them. Soon we were looking over their house at Southwater. I thought that when we saw it we would know immediately whether it was the one for us but we remained uncertain.

That night, after Stephen and Paul had gone to bed, Timothy asked us if we would minister to his wife. For several years Sarah had suffered from arthritis and her neck was so stiff that she could hardly turn it. Her knees and ankles were affected as well.

The following day we returned to Merston, and the moment we arrived home I was totally convinced that the house in Southwater was the right one for us.

Eventually Timothy rang.

'I've had others interested in the house,' he explained, 'but I know it's right for you to rent it. Before you visited us I asked the Lord to give me a sign if you were to be the next tenants. I said, "Lord, if you want John and Chris to live in my house, please heal Sarah through them." Two days after you came, the osteopath confirmed that Sarah's neck was almost completely normal. Praise the Lord!

'So that was the mysterious reason the Lord said would become apparent!' I said to John afterwards.

He laughed. 'It's a good job we didn't know about Timothy's prayer while we were there!' he said.

We journeyed to Horsham once more before moving there. Stephen had to attend an interview for a year's qualifying course at Horsham School of Art. There were a hundred applicants but only thirty places, so we were thrilled when he was accepted. And because we had travelled so far he was told the good news straight away.

We returned to Merston, and as we were preparing for the move the Lord showed us: 'I am sending you to a desert area. Fruit will appear in the desert, and there will be more bundles of gladness in the autumn. But look *ahead* all the time.'

Soon after the Lord had said these words we learned from

Trevor Dearing that he had been offered a living in the United States.

'If Anne and I decide to go,' Trevor said to John, would you like me to hand over my mailing list to you? I don't know of another couple in the U.K. doing such a similar work to ours.'

We were delighted at this offer, and felt privileged. Not everyone on Trevor's list of nearly a thousand people would wish to support us, but we could see how many might, and how the Lord could use this to fulfil his promise of widening and developing our ministry.

We had already arranged to move in June and such was the Lord's timing that the Dearings moved to America the same month, leaving the list in our hands.

The Huddersfield Examiner carried a full report about our impending move and the extension of our work. This was accompanied by a large photograph. The Lord had fulfilled his promise to vindicate us in the area. We reproduced the article in a newsletter sent to everyone on Trevor's mailing list as well as ours.

The Lord showed John that the Friday group would continue in the hands of a new leader, and that 'Breath Fellowship' would become the umbrella title for all our supporters everywhere.

Local ministers commissioned us at our Farewell Service, and a few days later we set off for the sunny south. Our bright yellow estate car was packed full of belongings that we had crammed in at the last moment. Heather and Rachel stood in the middle of the road waving their goodbyes and all along the street others popped out of their houses to wave too.

Our new home was on a quiet suburban estate at one end of Southwater village. When we arrived, Sarah and Timothy had brewed a welcome cup of tea for us in the small kitchen. The sun was streaming through the French windows in the through-lounge. This was already tastefully furnished, so we were able to sit down and relax before unpacking.

Outside in the small garden we could see red roses in full bloom, and beyond that cows grazing lazily in the field. The boys shot upstairs to arrange their belongings in the bedroom which they would have to share, since John needed the smallest one for his study.

When Sarah and Timothy had gone, John and I fell into each other's arms.

'Isn't it a lovely place!' he exclaimed.

'Yes,' I said happily, 'and I'm so thankful to be back in the south. It's just like coming home!'

Very soon after we moved in we began to receive many telephone calls from all over the country. Our post also increased considerably. People were sometimes prepared to travel long distances to receive ministry from us, though wherever possible we put them in touch with somebody who could help them in their own area.

Brenda felt it worth travelling the long journey from Bristol to see us on her day off.

'I haven't slept properly for months,' she said, 'as I've had a recurring nightmare. I think it's because I worked in a nursing home run by spiritists. When people died there the staff would make comments like, "I can see her mother standing beside the bed!"—and this frightened me.'

We prayed for Brenda, and she went home peacefully. A few weeks later she rang to say that she had experienced no more nightmares since we had ministered to her.

We still travelled long distances to take meetings, but we limited our visits to individuals to within a twenty-five mile radius of our new home.

So we would have been unable to go to London to visit Monica, a Christian lady living in Kensington. But she also owned a holiday home at Rustington, on the West Sussex coast, and there we ministered to her. Her disease of the eyelids had been diagnosed as incurable, and she feared that it might ultimately lead to blindness. Antibiotics and steroids had been prescribed for her to take indefinitely, and medically she could be helped no further.

We began ministering on a regular monthly basis and within a few months she had not only improved but was gradually able to come off all her tablets.

Her condition then stabilized. Each time that we ministered there was some improvement but before we were due to visit Monica again she would experience a slight deterioration. Once or twice she waited longer than usual before calling upon us and at such times her condition appeared to worsen. But whenever we laid hands on her the Lord brought her back to the point of stability that she had enjoyed before.

We've found that in cases like Monica's, people are able to receive a measure of healing but their further progress is restricted because of reasons which have not yet come to light. But eventually we traced the root cause of her problem to a fall many years previously when she had dislocated her neck. As we persisted with ministry for this she passed the point of stabilization and moved on towards complete healing.

On other occasions a condition will stabilize but then retreat. After we had ministered to a lady with stomach cancer, X rays showed that the cancer had stopped in its tracks and then gradually diminished.

One day at Southwater Paul was chatting to a boy who lived near the top of our road. The boy said that his father Daniel was interested in healing and asked if we had any books on the subject. We lent him some and later Daniel brought them back to our house.

'I have nasty headaches,' he told us. 'I was wondering whether you would pray for me.'

We laid hands on him and afterwards he shared how he had received ministry from the vicar at Shipley church.

'That's three miles out in the country,' Daniel explained. 'I'm sure he'd be interested to meet you.'

So one evening we went to look at the church and met Oswald, the vicar, and his wife Bunty. We had so much in common that we talked for hours. Until then we had had no idea where we would be worshipping locally, but during the evening Oswald invited John to assist him at the Sunday service. So from then on we worshipped at Shipley when we were free, and John preached there regularly until Oswald retired the following year.

Shortly after we had moved, the West Sussex County

Times had carried an article about us. Violet, a jeweller's wife who lived in Horsham, had read this with great interest. She suffered from arthritis and had tried various means of help without success. When we visited her in her home we used soaking prayer on her and she could feel the Lord's power flowing through my hands as I ministered to her ankles. Afterwards, while we were all chatting together, she turned to John and asked politely, 'Do you do healing too?'

John looked slightly taken aback.

'Yes, I do,' he replied, winking at me. 'But Jesus is the healer—we're the channels.'

As we left, Violet remarked, 'I'm so surprised you're both so normal!'

We all laughed.

Later Violet rang us with encouraging news.

'I've had the first day completely free of pain that I can remember,' she said cheerfully. 'Can you come and give me another dose?'

When we went this time, Violet told us about the many people she knew she thought would also benefit from our ministry.

'I wish I could gather them all in this room,' she declared enthusiastically, 'then you could touch them! Perhaps you'd like to hold a meeting here sometime?'

In the autumn we took up Violet's suggestion and fifty people packed into her lounge for the first of our meetings in Horsham. Later we held regular healing services in the Town Hall.

On Boxing Day Violet invited us to supper in her home. All her grown-up children were there, together with their families.

We looked forward to a relaxing evening. But while we were sampling the delicious food one daughter drew me aside.

'D'you think you could pray for me? I've had a bad back for a long time,' she confided.

We went upstairs and I ministered to her. Before I had finished, John was waiting with somebody else at the door and after we had finished with him, yet another person asked to see us.

When we eventually returned downstairs a little girl was pushed towards us by her parents, who stated, 'She has asthma.' So we ministered to her in the corridor!

As we laughed about it on our way out Violet said apologetically, 'I honestly didn't arrange the evening for you to come and cure all our family's ills!'

But in practice we discovered that once it leaked out that we laid hands on people for healing we were never off duty.

One day I was in a large, fashionable dress shop in Horsham. I had previously seen a blouse there that I liked and Stephen had promised to buy me a skirt to match it. I took the garments into the changing room to try them on, then went back into the shop to observe how they looked in the full-length mirror.

A sales lady came over, and after she had admired my prospective purchases we started chatting.

'I'm in absolute agony with my back!' she declared. 'I think I must have pulled a muscle. It's just there where it hurts.' She pointed to the spot.

To my surprise I heard myself saying confidently, 'If you let me lay my hand on it you'll feel heat and the pain will go.'

I placed my hand on her back and talked to her about Jesus and how he used to heal the sick.

'I can feel the heat coming into me!' she exclaimed. After a while the pain completely disappeared and she became very excited.

'This lady's cured my back!' she announced loudly to the other shop assistants. This caused quite a stir and the other customers couldn't help overhearing. A woman who was standing in the queue immediately piped up: 'You'd better come and do something for my hip!'

I realized that if I stayed much longer in the shop I would be inundated with requests for healing, so gathering up my purchases I made a hasty retreat.

Another day while out shopping I was offered a casual job in a greengrocer's shop to assist the staff during holiday periods and times of illness.

I enjoyed working there, but after a while life became so hectic that I asked the Lord whether I should leave. He showed me that it was not the right time yet.

However, after six months I knew that the time had come, so I gave a week's notice to Thelma, the acting manageress. The day before I was due to leave I noticed a young woman come into the shop with her baby. She was very upset as she spoke to Thelma and followed her through to the back of the shop. Soon it was time for my coffee break and I went out to where they were standing among the boxes of fruit and vegetables.

'Ah, here comes Chris!' Thelma said to the woman. 'She'll be able to help you. Her husband's a vicar.' She introduced us. 'This is Gillian—she thinks her house is haunted. I'll take over on the till while you two talk.'

I quickly poured my coffee. There was not much room but we both found stools to perch on and then Gillian explained: 'I'm not a very religious person and I don't know what to do. My father recently had a tragic accident. He was working on his car from underneath and it fell on him and killed him. When I saw him in the funeral parlour he was still bruised and afterwards in the street I kept seeing his face imprinted on everyone I looked at.' She started crying.

'Was it after seeing your father that you felt frightened?' I asked gently.

She nodded. 'I lie on my sofa in the daytime and shake all over and at night I can't sleep. I feel there's somebody watching me all the time. Would you be able to tell if my house was haunted if you came to it?'

'Yes,' I assured her. 'We've been called out before to houses with evil atmospheres. As you're so desperate, would you like us to come tonight?'

Gillian's face lit up. She explained where she lived, then left the shop. As I returned to the till, Thelma said, 'Gillian used to work here but I've never known her in such a state. She's normally a very cheerful person.'

As soon as we entered the house that evening I knew that it

was not haunted. For two hours we talked with Bibles open to Gillian and her husband, Then we laid hands on her and encouraged her to picture Jesus standing beside her father's coffin. As we prayed she felt something lift and experienced a sensation of floating. Afterwards she said with astonishment, 'However hard I try, I cannot see my father's face any more. All I can see is a cross.'

When Gillian called in at the shop several days later, she told Thelma that her fears had vanished.

16

'Take Out Your Keys'

We'll just have to get away for a break some time this year,' said John in a definite tone of voice. 'It's essential, now that the ministry's developing.'

I turned from watering a large plant in one corner of the lounge.

'Well, it won't be easy to scrape the money together,' I said candidly. 'We may be able to manage a self-catering holiday, though.'

As the weeks went by I had an impression of Bournemouth, where I had worked in a Christian guest house before we were married. But I became less certain about the self-catering idea.

One evening we were praying about it together and I had the word 'Elisha'. I shared this with John.

'Thank you, Lord!' he exclaimed in a loud voice. 'That settles it!' Then as I looked puzzled he explained: 'A few minutes ago I had the words "Bed and Breakfast, six nights". But I didn't mention it, as I thought it might be just my own desires—I'd rather have Bed and Breakfast than a self-catering holiday!

'Now what you don't know, darling, is that I'm in the middle of preparing a message on Elisha for a meeting in London. It's from that passage where he's given a room with a table, a chair, a bed and a lamp (2 Kings 4:10) and is waited upon by the Shunammite woman.

'The Lord knew that if he gave you "Elisha" it would confirm to me about the bed and breakfast. I suggest we book up for six nights at Bournemouth in the school holidays.'

So that is what we decided to do. In the meantime John went happily back to his study to continue working on the talk. He often spent many hours in preparation for the meetings but generally he enjoyed doing this.

He had been invited to give teach-ins at a Bible college and a London Healing Mission conference, as well as at our missions and other gatherings. Often he would speak from a scripture passage, giving instances of blessing from our own experience. But recently his longing to share about healing in particular had grown more intense, and one day while we were staying in Shropshire to take a mission there, John realized what the Lord wanted from him.

A canal wound its way through the pleasant countryside and we had sat down on the bank near a stone bridge to eat our packed lunch. Every so often a boat would come drifting or chugging along from one direction or the other.

As we finished our lunch I had the thumps and the Lord said to John, 'I want you to teach more about healing and to help people go further into healing.' He indicated that in his talks John was usually to speak about healing in some way, and to train other Christians to minister it. John saw this as referring to all areas: salvation (healing of spirit), physical healing, inner healing (of mind, will and emotions), deliverance, restoring of relationships, and the wholeness that results from leading balanced lives.

At the same time the Lord confirmed that he would develop my own ministry and I had an impression that I would be doing lots and lots of writing. He also said that we were engaged in an interim ministry—which was necessary and useful—but he would shortly bring to birth the third and widest of the ministries which he had promised us.

As soon as we returned home, some of these things began to happen.

One day a Pentecostal pastor made an interesting remark when he invited John to speak at his church.

'I've been there for over twenty years,' he said, 'and we've had ministry for healing at our services regularly. But I cannot say that we've had very much success in this area when you consider how long we've been doing it. Could we be missing out on something?'

John replied that he wasn't sure. But the pastor's observation tied in with something which the Lord had been impressing on my husband in a fresh way: that faith is not the only key to healing and that the absence of other vital keys might 'restrict the flow'.

When we took a mission in a northern city John spoke at the different meetings on 'Six keys to healing'. In the middle of the mission the chap who had invited us remarked, 'I never realized there was so much to the subject as this! Why don't you sell the cassettes of these talks? There must be many folk like me who need to hear this teaching.'

Then on the last evening, during the hymn before his message, John heard the Lord speaking to him: 'Take out your keys.'

He removed the ring of keys from his trouser pocket and noticed for the first time that there were six on it. He drew the attention of the congregation to this as he began to preach.

Afterwards the idea for our first six cassettes began to take shape. John had noticed something more: a definite correlation between each key on his ring and each key that he had preached about.

First there was his front door key. Faith, he believed, was the front door key to healing, while unbelief could hinder it. This became the subject for the first cassette.

Secondly there was his back door key. This represented the guidance of the Holy Spirit. God's prompting and guiding needs to be behind the ministry for healing or it will prove ineffective.

A third key fitted the fuel tank in our car. The lock on this was generally hidden from view and this reminded John that love is often the key to our innermost problems. Lack of love, in contrast, might hold up the healing.

Next came the garage key, and John recalled how tools are

often kept in the garage. The gifts of the Spirit had become vital tools without which we couldn't exercise our ministry.

Then there was the ignition key to our car—speaking to us of power, the key to spiritual ignition. We had experienced some meetings where there was faith and love yet the power was not released through praise, gifts or ministry.

The remaining key on my husband's ring fitted every door in the car, including the boot lid and the cubby hole. Without this key we were unable to get into our vehicle, let alone to move forward in it. John saw a willingness to change as the key to Christian progress; sometimes it is necessary for complete wholeness.

As well as sharing about the keys, he often encouraged people to take 'one step forward' at the meetings.

A lady called Kay did some late-night shopping one evening. On the way home she decided to pop in for about fifteen to thirty minutes to the church when we were holding a service. Later Kay told us: 'I'd only been there a few minutes and I knew from the interpretation of a tongue that I'd be there for the evening! The Lord had already been speaking to me the previous week about my need to stop playing about in shallow water and go forward into the deeper water—though I wasn't sure what this meant. Then I heard him say at the service that he wanted to lead me gently into new depths, and from then on the whole meeting spoke to me on this theme.

'I decided to take one step forward with him, into the deeper water, and accordingly came forward for prayer. I was still not sure what it all meant, but very much wanted to do it and was thirsting to go on. When we sang the song "Launch out into the deep" it was so meaningful.'

While people like Kay were moving one step forward, others were taking steps of a different kind which would play a part in the development of our ministry.

One of these was Lily, an elderly lady who worshipped at Shipley. She came to our meetings at Horsham Town Hall and there one night we ministered to her for her pain. At the close of the service the pain was still there, but by the time she arrived home it had completely disappeared.

Lily contacted a friend in East Grinstead who was a police-woman and told her about us. Soon Teresa was coming to the Town Hall meetings when she was off duty.

One day I had a long chat with her over the phone.

'I do wish you'd come and hold a meeting at East Grinstead!' she said ardently.

'Well, we can't just come and say "here we are",' I laughed. 'But if you can get a group of people together who want us we'll come.'

Not long afterwards Teresa rang again.

'I've found about a dozen who are interested,' she said brightly. 'If you give me a date I'll book the parish hall and get some publicity going.'

Her hopes were more than fulfilled. We held the meeting and about seventy people packed into the hall. Before the service began we were approached by Norman, a local Methodist minister.

'I want you to know that we're right behind you in what you're doing,' he said with a beaming smile.

Half-way through the evening a young couple brought their ten month old baby to be prayed for.

'Rebecca has a discharge from her ears,' they explained. 'It's been going on for some time and the doctors say that if it doesn't clear up soon they'll have to operate.'

Everyone was quiet and uniting in prayer as we laid hands on the child and prayed.

In a few days the discharge had cleared up and the opera-tion was unnecessary. The little girl was so obviously better that a neighbour noticed and Rebecca's parents were able to speak to her about Jesus. She accepted him and there she was at our next service in East Grinstead!

This was held in Norman's church, and from then on we went there regularly.

Norman was editor of the Methodist Revival Fellowship magazine *Sound of Revival*, and one day he invited John to submit an article entitled 'He heals today'. The result was further requests for our meetings and ministry. And when the article was reproduced in the *Flame* we were inundated with prayer requests for sick people, especially from Northern Ireland. Our normal policy was to pray for such people during our meetings and then pass their names on to our intercessors' groups in different parts of the country.

We were interested to notice that sometimes we had a 'run' on one particular need. This could be so predictable that if the phone rang during that period we guessed what it was about! For a while the predominant problem might be skin disease, then it could change to rheumatism. After that it might be heart trouble. When it was foot complaints I was perpetually kneeling on the floor to minister. Someone suggested that I should have worked in a shoe shop!

We were pleased that the Hickstead show-jumping course was not far from where we lived. One day we went there with the boys to watch one of the championships. Most of the leading international show jumpers were taking part and the event was being televised. Crowds of adults and children had come to enjoy a day out. Stephen and Paul were excited about meeting the top riders and clamoured to obtain their autographs.

During an interval John and I walked arm in arm around the perimeter of the course, away from the horses and riders waiting to enter the arena. We wandered among the many stalls and the rows of parked cars.

'Do you remember,' John recalled, 'what the Lord said about training people to minister healing? I feel I want to get going on that soon.'

'Well,' I said thoughtfully, 'I'm sure there must be some Christians in every place who'd be interested. Wouldn't it be good if one day we could have a healing centre? We could hold a clinic for ministry and conferences for training.'

'Perhaps the Lord will provide a house for that eventually,' said John, 'but right now we could begin with particular days somewhere and see how they go.'

'East Grinstead would be a good place to start,' I suggested.

'That's what I was thinking. It's fairly central for people in the south-east to travel to. I'm sure Norman would be happy about it and we know that there are some in the churches there who want to go deeper into healing.' We turned and strolled back to the arena. 'We could spend a whole day on each of the keys alone,' John continued. 'There are so many practical questions that people are asking.'

The boys rejoined us and we were soon engrossed in watching the next event.

In the autumn of that year eighty Christians enjoyed the first of our training days at East Grinstead and these were followed, by popular request, with six similar days each year. They were specifically 'for those wishing to share the healing love of Jesus', and were held on Saturdays from mid-morning to late afternoon.

During the worship, the Lord invariably spoke through the gifts of the Spirit. There were lively periods of sharing, questions and discussion and at the last session of each day John encouraged people to minister to one another. Some stepped out in doing this for the first time.

In his talks John explored such practical questions as: 'How should we pray for the sick?' 'Should we expect instant results?' 'When should I lay hands on someone?' and 'How can I share the gifts of the Spirit with a sick person?'

Christians travelled from near and far. Gale, from Essex, wrote to say how one such day had particularly helped her:

I remember you saying that we must step out in faith, using the gifts Jesus will give us at the time of need. A friend of mine had to go into hospital for another fairly minor operation. She had already had four big operations, also a lot of bronchitis—and she has recently suffered pleurisy. Consequently anaesthetics were always a considerable risk. I felt, surely this is a situation where I must go to her and offer to pray for her.

We asked the Lord to heal her lungs, and to care for her during the operation. We thanked him for it. She had the operation, and the surgeon said when he examined her that he could not believe that she had just recovered from pleurisy! After the anaesthetic she felt so well, no coughing or difficult breathing as was usually the case. So praise the Lord! Had it not been for the training session I probably would not have gone to her.

Similar sentiments have been expressed by others attending the training days, and they continue to be major dates in our calendar.

We were glad to hear of individuals like Gale who put into practice what they learned from us. And we were particularly encouraged when leaders started healing services in their churches as a result of our ministry.

A lady who travelled regularly from London to our Horsham meetings had suffered terrible pain in her foot but after several sessions of the laying on of hands it was completely better. Her husband was delighted, for they could now go out for walks together again. At his suggestion we were invited to minister at their church.

On this occasion John went alone. The church had no experience of the healing ministry but John had been asked to speak about it. He wondered whether anyone at all would come forward for the laying on of hands. But over half the multi-racial congregation stayed at the communion rail and he was ministering to them long after the service had officially ended.

The following year we were invited again, and this time we both went to the church. As soon as we arrived, a man approached John.

'You prayed for me last year,' he said, 'and since then I've had no epileptic fits.'

'That's great!' John said.

After the service an informal discussion took place and we were asked many questions. There was a strong desire to continue this sort of ministry in the church there. And within a few weeks we heard that the two ministers had incorporated the laying on of hands into the regular worship.

Another strand in the development of our ministry had begun just before our first Christmas at Southwater. Trevor Dearing came over to this country and was due to speak at a large interdenominational renewal meeting in Tunbridge Wells.

For a long time I had felt there was something particularly significant about Tunbridge Wells in relation to our ministry, and the Lord showed us that we had at all costs to be there for this rally.

The church where it was to be held was only a few miles from where my parents and sisters lived and when they heard that we were planning to be at the meeting they wanted to come, too.

When the day arrived we awoke to see a thick carpet of snow on the ground. We looked at it in dismay, for a journey by car would be treacherous. So we decided to go by train if the weather didn't improve. This would mean buying sleeping bags on the way and staying overnight at my parents' house.

By late afternoon the conditions had worsened. So John and I trudged through the snow with our cases to catch the bus to Horsham.

Paul had had a cookery class at school and when he emerged he was clutching a tin containing a chocolate log for Christmas, so we had to cart that with us, too! We met Stephen in the town centre and purchased our sleeping bags. Then, complete with luggage, we trailed over a mile to the railway station.

As we clambered into a compartment I breathed an audible sigh.

'We must be stark raving mad!' I exclaimed.

17

Full Circle

When we reached Tunbridge Wells most events in the town had been cancelled because of the weather. But the rally was still on and approximately three hundred people had managed to get there. When the ministry time came, Trevor asked us to assist him with the laying on of hands. And afterwards we had the first clue about why it had been necessary for us to be there: John was invited to speak at a later date.

The following April we all made the trip again, this time under easier circumstances. After the service we received three offers.

First Lawrence, who had recorded the service, offered to copy our cassettes regularly on his high speed equipment. Later we were also to use his computer to produce the address labels for our mailing list. Both these machines saved us much time.

The second offer was an invitation to minister occasionally at a meeting in Southborough. This brought back memories for me when I discovered that it was held in my old school. And we gathered for prayer beforehand in my classroom!

The third offer came from Graham, the organist. He was prepared to play his electronic organ at our rallies if we should need him. We were delighted. He has since played at many of our gatherings and his music has enhanced them.

Graham enthused about our ministry to his church elders

at Eastbourne and as a result we were invited there to minister in his chapel. John and I went for a Sunday in the autumn. After the morning service we learned that we were to have lunch with a couple called Geoff and Geraldine. Geoff was a director of Kingsway Publications. In the car on the way to their house Geraldine asked us, 'How did you come into this ministry?'

'That's a long story,' I replied. 'But if you're interested we'll tell you later.'

For some while before this visit to Eastbourne I had been seeing in my mind a slightly open door. The first time that I saw it I described it to John and he said that it sounded Edwardian. I had also had an impression of a large, homely fireplace.

After we entered Geoff's house John asked him how old it was.

'It's Edwardian,' he answered.

And a distinctive feature of the room which we were in was a fireplace similar to the one that I had seen!

As we chatted we were surprised to discover that Geoff used to attend the same school as John in Tonbridge!

Then, after lunch, and for much of the afternoon, we related the story of our experiences. As we drew to a close, Geoff was leaning forward in his chair.

'You know,' he said, 'what you've been telling us is publishable material....'

'Perhaps we weren't so mad after all when we made that journey in the snow!' I reflected.

That winter journey to Tunbridge Wells was not the only occasion when John and I had a struggle to get to a meeting. We were due to minister one evening at an Anglican church in London. But during the day both of us quite suddenly were afflicted with severe pain. John could hardly move his back and I couldn't turn my neck. As the time drew near when we were due to leave home I struggled to change my blouse, but cried out in agony, and had to forgo the idea. I sat on the bed in tears.

'I can't go!' I said to John.

'Oh yes you can!' he assured me. 'Let's minister to one another and trust the Lord.'

We did, but the pains remained. So John said, 'I'll make you a hot water bottle and you can hold it against your neck during the journey.'

A little while later John hobbled out to the car followed by me clutching my hot water bottle. As we set off I chuckled and remarked, 'We hardly look the picture of health to be taking a healing service!'

When we reached the outskirts of London we decided to change drivers so that John could consult the map and give me instructions where to go. But I cried out every time I turned my head and John had to hold the hot water bottle against my neck for me.

It so happened that we were on the outside lane of the carriageway. And just as we approached the sign pointing to where we should have turned off, a high lorry obscured our view and we missed the turning. So then we were travelling in the wrong direction, in the busy rush hour, on a road that it seemed impossible to leave. We eventually did find a turning off, but then we were lost and already it was past the time for the meeting to begin.

When we found the district where the church was situated we could not find the church! Everyone that we asked was very helpful and we attempted to follow their instructions, but we ended up in the middle of a housing estate with no church anywhere in sight!

At last, rather frustrated, we found it. Several people were outside, looking anxiously for us.

'Praise the Lord!' said one of the men when he spotted us. 'We've been praying you here.'

The large church was full of people and the vicar immediately handed over the meeting to John.

When it came to the ministry of laying on of hands I noticed Barbara at the front of the queue, the lady from Woodford whose hearing had been restored through John. As she explained to me what *she* needed ministry for, I asked if she wouldn't mind laying hands on *me* first!

A little later John walked down the aisle to minister to a woman in a wheelchair and called me over to help. She slumped back in the spirit, but as we turned away we heard a commotion. I swung round just in time to observe a bald-headed lady in her wheelchair endeavouring to retrieve from the floor a hat with a wig attached to it! I glanced at her face and was relieved to see that she obviously considered the incident amusing.

When the service was over John said to me, 'That's strange! My pain disappeared completely during the ministry, but it's back again now.'

I laughed. 'My pain went too,' I told him, 'but now I can't turn my head again!'

It was several days before these troubles disappeared for good.

We don't attribute all such difficulties to Satan! However, we feel that he sometimes tries to prevent us from getting to meetings. And on very rare occasions he nearly succeeds in disrupting them.

Once, at another rally in London, a Christian woman gave a 'prophecy'. It was couched in religious phraseology but delivered in a wailing tone and I quickly discerned that it was not from the Lord.

We were in an Anglican church, and after the woman had sat down the vicar stood up to say that he thought that the 'gift' should be tested. A number of folk in the congregation raised their hands to agree that God had not spoken. Then John swiftly encouraged people to turn their eyes back to Jesus.

On another occasion, during a healing service at a Pentecostal church in the Midlands, a lady gave a gift of tongues. Immediately John saw a picture of a fireplace. But at the same moment a coloured man screeched out an interpretation in very emotional tones. It included quotations from Scripture and mention of the blood of the Lamb. But I discerned that it was motivated by a religious evil spirit. It left many of us feeling cold and we found it difficult to get back into an atmosphere of worship.

The pastor was leading this part of the service, and when he eventually handed over to John my husband shared how he had seen a fireplace with coals in the grate but no fire. It was a picture of the church there. God was calling people to return to him before he would rekindle the fire of his Spirit in that place.

Following this, John called on me to give the Bible reading. But, before I did, I told the congregation that I believed John's fireplace was the *true* interpretation of the tongue given earlier in the service.

After the meeting we asked the pastor about the coloured man.

'Oh, he *often* comes out with words like that,' was the reply.

I explained that I thought the coloured man needed deliverance and the pastor agreed.

'But he won't hear of it,' he said. 'He doesn't think there's anything wrong with him.'

'Well, you're going to have constant trouble here unless the man is either delivered or asked to leave,' John said solemnly.

Again the pastor agreed. 'He's already been thrown out of two other churches!' he told us.

We left the matter in the pastor's hands.

As we continued the ministry from our base at Southwater I experienced a restlessness that went on for several months. I felt that I was being led to take up something new, but I was not at all sure what. I knew that it involved lots and lots of writing, yet it encompassed more than working with John on this book. It had to do with studying and with my hands. And I expected that it would complement the ministry that I was doing already. The desire to get started was very strong and I had several conversations with John about what it could be.

I scanned the local newspaper for details of evening classes, but was not specially attracted to any of the subjects offered. So I tentatively approached the local careers' office to enquire about the possibilities for a woman of forty.

I was given a pile of leaflets describing various therapies, but the one that stood out from them all was osteopathy, the treatment of certain diseases and abnormalities by manipulating bones and muscles. I had always been fascinated by the human body, avidly devouring any information that I could obtain about it. I had learned so much through the healing ministry, but I longed to increase my knowledge. I felt thrilled at the prospect of using my hands for the Lord in this additional way.

I immediately contacted the British School of Osteopathy in London to find out what qualifications I should need and was invited there for an informal interview.

But before this I was due to go into hospital for a minor operation. I couldn't sleep the night before and I was surprised that I was so worried about it. But once in hospital I was examined and told that I needed a more major operation than expected: I was to have a laparotomy, an investigation performed by inserting a tube into the abdomen. Somewhat alarmed I wondered whether there was anything seriously wrong with me. After my pre-med I said to the Lord, 'Please give me something to hold on to.'

Straight away came again the still, small voice: 'Jude.'

Dreamily, and with some effort, I reached for my Bible and turned to the letter of Jude. My eyes focussed on four words in the first verse: '*Kept* for Jesus Christ.'

'Thank you, Lord!' I whispered as I lay my head back on my pillow.

After the operation I was told that everything was perfectly normal and that there was nothing to worry about.

John coped marvellously with the house and boys while I was in hospital, but they were all pleased to have me home again.

It was not long afterwards that John had his final check-up on the place where his malignant mole had been removed and was pronounced clear. With some relief we praised the Lord for his keeping power.

When my appointment came round at the osteopathy college I was interviewed by the vice-principal. I learned that it would take something like seven years for me to

IT HURTS TO HEAL

qualify. I should need to pass several science examinations before embarking upon a four-year course at the college as a day student.

I didn't mind how long it would take. I was just glad that I could begin to work towards my objective. Somehow I would have to fit in my studies alongside the ministry. But it's surprising what you can do when the Lord calls you!

When I returned home Paul reminded me that I had promised to take him to Guildford during his half-term holiday. I drove him there soon afterwards and we spent an enjoyable afternoon shopping. Then we made our way back to the open air car park beside the river.

To our dismay the car wouldn't start. The engine was completely dead. I ran to a nearby garage to ask for help, but all the mechanics were out. So I searched for a phone box and after three calls succeeded in obtaining a promise of assistance. A man eventually got the car going, but it was a twenty mile journey home, and I was concerned all the way in case it should break down again.

That evening John and I had a long discussion about the car. It had already let us down several times and because we travelled so much we were constantly spending out on repairs. So we decided to look for a newer one.

Among the vehicles on display outside a garage in Horsham was a bright red Morris, which we both came to believe was the one for us. But immediately we stepped into the sales room I was overwhelmed by a heaviness which indicated to me that something was not right. Then, when we made enquiries, we were disappointed at the low amount offered us on our old vehicle. So we decided to leave it a while and look elsewhere.

Whenever we passed that garage in the next few weeks we looked hopefully for the red car. And always, although others were sold, that one remained.

'Either there must be something wrong with it,' John commented, 'or the Lord's keeping it for us.'

Eventually we came to the conclusion tht it was time to return and try again. On this occasion a different salesman approached us and we explained that we had no cash, but if a deal could be worked out on paper we were interested in the red Morris.

'We were wondering, though,' John added, 'why it's been outside so long without being sold?'

'Ah, we nearly did sell it twice,' explained the salesman. 'Two other people very much wanted it but couldn't afford the deposit.' Then he consulted his book and offered us nearly three hundred pounds more on our old car than the other salesman had done. This was sufficient for *our* deposit. After we had been for a test drive he also offered to obtain a reduction in our monthly payments for the new vehicle! Two satisfied customers later collected the car and drove away in it.

As we drove home we recalled our first visit to the garage.

'Right car, wrong time, wasn't it?' John said.

We were unable to park the car in our own garage straight away because we had allowed the boys to play snooker there with their friends.

Since qualifying at art school Stephen had benefited from two training courses and was at the time doing temporary work in the Horsham area. He and Paul, at eighteen and fifteen, seemed to have suddenly shot up, and were taller than both of us.

Although the house had been furnished, we had brought the boys' beds with us from Merston. But these were only two feet six inches wide and they had outgrown them long ago. Whenever I was making them I wished they had larger ones.

One morning, somewhat frustrated, I had a conversation with the Lord about it: 'Can't you do something about these beds, Lord? The boys must be terribly uncomfortable in them.'

Within a week we received a telephone call from a lady who had recently moved to Tunbridge Wells and to whom we had ministered not long before.

'We have some furniture to dispose of,' she said, 'and I had an impression of you. Do you need any beds?'

'Yes, we do!' I shouted down the phone, 'desperately!'

177

'Well, we've got two three foot single beds you can have if we can manage to get them to you.'

Quite soon afterwards a young man from her church brought them over in his van. As they were unloaded I gasped with delight.

'They're beautiful!' I exclaimed.

The beds were luxurious and in perfect condition.

On his way out the man asked us, 'What have you done with your old ones?'

'John put them outside,' I answered. 'The council will have to take them away.'

'I'll take them off your hands,' the man declared. 'I know a very poor family who'd be extremely grateful for them.'

As he drove the van away I was over the moon with pleasure, and we thanked the Lord for answering my prayer.

We went upstairs to admire the beds again and John put his arm around me.

'There's only one problem,' he said, glancing at the cluttered surroundings. 'The boys have even less room to move now than before.'

This was true. In fact, we were all feeling rather cramped. We were definitely in the house of the Lord's choice, but it was particularly difficult with two teenagers when people came for ministry and when we had major office tasks to do, like sending out the newsletter. The study was too small for this, so for several days meals were disrupted as we took over the dining table in the lounge.

Soon after moving to Southwater I had been shown by the Lord that we would be in the house for three years, until Paul had completed his schooling. And John had seen a picture of roses, signifying that our next move would be during the summer.

Now Paul was in his final year at school, and we began to trust the Lord for a larger house. We were particularly drawn to Kent, and to the Tunbridge Wells area, where we originally came from.

One confirmation that the Lord was leading in this direction came as I pursued my studies. After we had moved

I would need to continue the course that I had started. But I suddenly learned that very few day colleges provided a course in Human Biology at advanced level. I made extensive enquiries and could find only one in the whole of Kent, and that was in Tonbridge!

As we looked forward towards yet another move, we heard from Trevor Dearing that he was going to resume his ministry in this country. Our connection with him had given our work a tremendous impetus, but now we handed back his mailing list. However, our ministry was developing, widening and changing as the Lord had promised, and we wondered what further changes our move to Kent would bring.

John was eager to take on any new challenge that lay ahead. He didn't know exactly where or how his gifts would be used in the future, but he was confident that the Lord would open fresh doors of opportunity for his ministry.

One autumn day we were due to minister at a rally in Hastings, and we decided to call in on the way at the college in Tonbridge to find out more about my course. I was told there that, provided I passed my exams and obtained a grant, I would be eligible for a place.

We had a few minutes to spare, so before resuming our journey we walked past John's old school and around the corner by St Stephen's church, where we were married.

'Do you remember what the vicar preached on at our wedding?' John asked. 'He gave us God's promise to Jacob: "I will keep you in *all places* wherever you go, and will *bring you back* to this land'—the area where he came from" (Genesis 28:15—authors' paraphrase).'

'Oh yes!' I exclaimed. 'Isn't it strange to think we're coming back here to live after twenty years! All *I* can remember is the vicar quoting the promise of Jesus: "Lo, I am with you all the days"—the glad days and the sad days.'

John squeezed my hand, and said softly, 'We'd no idea then just how many sad days we had in front of us. But he *has* been with us, and now we've come full circle.'

'We certainly have,' I thought, glancing across the road.

Opposite was the bus stop where our traumas had begun.

18

The Mystery Is Solved

After twelve months at Southborough, we were shown by the Lord to buy our own house, and we saw just the right one in Tonbridge, not far from John's parents, and in our original home parish, St Stephen's.

But there was a problem. We had no money, and we knew that because of our faith ministry it would not be easy to obtain a mortgage. Yet this did not stop John from making an offer, which was accepted, and very soon we saw a large notice outside the house: '*Under Offer*'. Every time I passed this I chuckled to myself. 'Lord,' I said, 'that's our offer and we haven't a penny towards it or a stick of furniture!'

But the Lord proved his faithfulness once again through his people. The mortgage was granted, loans were turned into gifts towards the deposit, and, although we purchased some items on credit, the majority were provided for by gifts in kind or cash.

It was another six months before we were able to move into what we now call Breath House, and the week before we did was exceptionally hectic. John had several meetings on and I had my mock exams. One day I had made my usual dash to the shops and had carried several heavy bags to the car. On the way home I was waiting for the traffic lights to change when I became suddenly aware that I had blacked out for a few seconds. It frightened me, though I felt fine afterwards, and when I shared this with John we decided it must have been due to stress, and promptly forgot about it.

During the summer I passed my exams for entrance to the British School of Osteopathy in the autumn term. I enjoyed commuting to London each day. The first year of the course required a detailed knowledge of anatomy, physiology and embryology. I found it fulfilling but overwhelming. The Lord said of it, 'It will be difficult, but from your doing this course will come great blessing to your joint ministry, and I will use you together more effectively as a result.'

With homework to do in the evenings and at weekends, I only had time to be involved in our local meetings, and we both felt unable to give regular private ministry or prayer counselling except to ministers and leaders when the Lord showed us.

We came to see that we were able to help far more people through John training other Christians to minister in these and all areas of healing. We were both excited at what the Lord was doing, though we longed to see more Christians mobilized to share the healing love of Jesus with people all around them, not just bringing his touch in meetings but in everyday life.

During the last few years there has been more demand for our Training Days, and John now holds regular ones in several places as well as being available to travel anywhere he's invited. Many of the insights shared at the days are reproduced in his book *Six Keys to Healing*

Training is also the emphasis of our conferences, which are always great times of fellowship. A lady from Worthing wrote to us, 'The thing about them is the love—the non-judging, non-critical, loving atmosphere, and the quiet peace.'

We have produced over a hundred worship and teaching cassettes, which have been requested by people all over the country and in different parts of the world. Some Christian groups use our cassettes in their meetings, and John sometimes supplies notes to guide them.

It was in the midst of an encouraging and fulfilling but expanding and eventful ministry like this that we had to face something we were quite unprepared for.

When I woke up on Sunday 7 December 1986 I had no idea that this was the day when the nightmare was going to recur. Everything seemed so normal, yet when I picked up the telephone to answer it around five o'clock in the afternoon, I had lived it all before.

'Christine,' my mother said, 'Rosemary's dead.'

'No!' I gasped. 'Not another one! How?'

'Ron's just rung from Australia,' she said flatly. 'They'd been sitting watching a film on TV. She got up, took two steps, and collapsed in his arms.'

'We'll be round right away,' I cried.

Rosemary had been thirty-eight, and had three lovely children. Our hearts ached for them, and for Ron—so far, far away.

At my parents' house we stared at each other in horror. A feeling of hopelessness pervaded the place. Was our family unique? Were we the only ones in the world to be affected by this? Whatever could it be, this thing that was striking us down one by one? As we left I felt angry that this had happened once again, and I said to myself, 'This time I'm going to fight it.'

Later that evening Mark and Lynda came to comfort us. John explained to them: 'Although various diagnoses have been made on the death certificates, no cause has ever really been found.'

'Ten years ago when my brother Paul died,' I added, 'they said medical science was not advanced enough to tell us why. But I'm determined to find the reason, because there must be one.' I started to cry, and Lynda took me in her arms.

'Well, let's make a cup of coffee,' suggested Mark, 'and then we'll pray.'

During the prayer time Lynda shared, 'I can see a golden key.' Then later as we talked she expanded on what she had seen. 'Although the key looked new,' she said slowly, 'I sense that really it's old.'

'That could mean,' I said thoughtfully, 'that we're not looking for something completely unknown to man. For some time I've wondered if it might be an abnormal heart rhythm that's only present at the time of death. This would explain why it hasn't been detected beforehand in ECGs or after death in post mortems.'

That night in bed I had the thumps and the Lord said through John, 'I will help you find the key, and enable you to turn it.'

A couple of days later I marched into our doctor's surgery. 'You are going to do something, aren't you?' I pleaded. 'Please don't let the rest of my family drop dead as well!' My voice broke as I said the words.

Dr Bowden looked at me evenly. 'I'll get you an appointment with a cardiologist,' he promised. 'If only we could obtain a record of the heart rhythm at the point of death,' he continued, 'it could tell us so much. But I expect it all happened too quickly again.'

I looked at him helplessly. 'What can cause the heart suddenly to go into a different rhythm?' I asked. 'In our case it would have to be congenital, wouldn't it?'

He reached for a pad. 'Look,' he said kindly, 'you understand enough about anatomy for me to explain one possibility.' He drew a rough sketch of the heart. 'Some people are born with an extra pathway for the electrical impulse to travel along—we call it an extra bundle.' He pointed to a spot. 'It's usually just there. If the impulse happens to travel along the pathway at the wrong second, the heart goes out of synchronization.'

'But if it was that,' I queried, 'surely it would show up in a post mortem?'

'Not necessarily. It's very minute.'

As the days went by we learned, without undue surprise, that the Australian doctor had written on Rosemary's death certificate 'Cause unknown'. We also learned that several times during the preceding year she had blacked out momentarily.

It began to dawn on me that I too had blacked out on one occasion, and, although it had seemed insignificant at the time, it now assumed great importance. Fear sometimes gripped me as I realized that the possibility of my having what had taken the others was getting more likely, and that Stephen and Paul might have it too.

John was very worried and upset as well. But, each time he came home from a meeting, he brought encouragement from Christians who had been praying for us. Many sent letters and messages to me about how the Lord was revealing to them that he had set me on my course.

Overwhelmed by the shock, grief and uncertainty of it all, I sobbed frequently in John's arms. 'He's not going to snatch you away in the middle of it, darling,' he constantly reassured me.

Several doctors that we spoke to during this period also gave me hope, especially in view of the tremendous progress made in the field of medicine since my brother Paul had died. But none of them could explain my blackout, and, in view of my family history, they believed that it could not be ignored. So seeing a cardiologist became an urgent necessity, yet it might be months before it would be possible.

One evening I was explaining all this on the telephone to my friend Fran in Alton when she remarked, 'Have you thought of going through St Luke's?' John and I knew about St Luke's Hospital in London, to which top consultants offer their services free to clergy and their dependants, but we had not thought of taking this course, which would be much quicker. Dr Bowden enthusiastically supported our decision to do so, with the result that, just one month after Rosemary's death, John and I found ourselves sitting in Dr P. H. Kidner's consulting room in St John's Wood.

Dr Kidner asked lots of questions, and I told him that I thought the deaths were due to a fault in the electrical conduction of the heart.

'Why do you think that?' he asked.

I shrugged. 'Well, it's the only thing left, isn't it?'

He looked at me thoughtfully. Then after we had been there an hour, and he had thoroughly examined me, he said confidently, 'The best way that I can help you is by sending you to my friend Dr Richard Sutton. He is an expert in the electrical conduction system of the heart.'

Not long afterwards we travelled to Harley Street for our appointment with Dr Sutton, who is a cardio-electrophysiologist, one of the few in this country. We were shown into his consulting room where he greeted us warmly from behind his desk. I looked at this tall slim doctor. My eyes were drawn to his dark suit, his silk tie and matching handkerchief, and I thought how smart he appeared. I instantly liked him, and was impressed by his calm, reassuring manner.

The moment that we sat down he said positively, 'It is irrefutable that you should have tests.'

'Well, I do hope you can help us discover what it is,' I said determinedly, 'because I'm prepared to travel the world until I found out.'

His eyes twinkled. 'You won't have to travel the world, Mrs Huggett. But the only way we can find out if anything is wrong is by inserting wires into your heart. This is unpleasant, and has to be done while you are awake.'

'That doesn't sound very nice!' I said apprehensively.

'What about the risks?' John enquired.

The doctor smiled. 'It's perfectly safe.'

'What if you don't find anything?' I asked.

'Then it means there is nothing wrong,' he declared. 'If it's there, we'll find it.'

'And what about treatment?'

'It depends on what we find. You may need a pacemaker, you may need drugs...we'll see. But I want you to come into Westminster Hospital as soon as possible, and I shall do the tests myself.'

After one-and-a-quarter hours in his consulting room I knew that I had met the man who was going to help us find the key and turn it.

On the way home John and I were caught in the rush hour. The tube train was packed, and we clung on to each other to avoid falling into the other passengers.

'I feel there's some hope at last, darling,' John said optimistically. He gave me a quick kiss on the cheek.

'Yes, that man inspires confidence. He obviously knows what he's talking about. I just want the time to go now so that we can get on with it.'

John nodded. 'The worst thing is all this uncertainty.' The train lurched, and I clung to my husband more tightly.

'I'm worried about my studies too,' I exclaimed. 'I'm already behind.'

'I know,' he said sympathetically, 'but this is a matter of life and death. I'm sure they will understand at the college.' Just then the doors opened, and we pushed our way out.

On a Monday evening a few weeks later I trudged with my case to the hospital. I entered a ward that was small and square, with about a dozen beds. Mine was at the far end by the window. The other ladies smiled and nodded at me as I walked briskly towards it. The atmosphere was happy and relaxed and I soon felt very much at home in Edgar Horne Ward. It wasn't long before I was sharing with everybody my reason for being there. Sheila, who was in the next bed to me, voiced the desire of them all when she said with feeling, 'I do hope they find it, Chris.'

I felt perfectly all right until the Tuesday evening, the night before I was due to have the tests. The women in the ward were gathered in groups chatting, but I sat brooding on my bed.

'I've got to prepare myself for what might happen,' I thought. 'Dr Sutton is going to try to induce in me the same condition that all four have died from. Can I be sure they will bring me back if I cut out? He said that the tests were very controlled, but what we have in our family is rare.

'Perhaps I'll have to have a pacemaker fitted. What will that be like for the rest of my life? The ladies in this ward with them think they are marvellous.

'How about if I have an extra bundle? Will it mean surgery?

'I might have to take tablets for the rest of my life. But all tablets have side-effects, don't they?

'And what if they find nothing? How will I cope with that? Especially as I had that blackout.'

My mind was in a turmoil, and I suddenly jumped up and blurted out, 'Where's the chapel?'

The ladies stopped their chatter. 'It's on the seventh floor,' said one of them. 'It's lovely and quiet up there.'

I hurried out of the ward and ran up the stairs.

When I entered the chapel I immediately felt the peace. I sat on a chair and started to pray aloud. 'We've been through a lot together, Lord, and now it's just you and me again. I'm in your hands. You know what's going to happen tomorrow. *Please* help us find the key.'

I stayed a while before returning to the ward in a much calmer state. It was still a long night, though.

John didn't get much sleep that night, either. He had been to visit me each day, and he had lots of people praying for me, but all the things that concerned me worried him too.

The next morning he busied himself with jobs in the house, as he was unable to concentrate on work for the ministry. As he boarded the midday train for London he still had two overriding prayers in his mind: 'Lord, just take care of Chris and bring her through. Lord, let them find something and help them to put it right.'

Meanwhile, I was undergoing the tests in the operating theatre, and from the start it was an amazing experience. Dr Sutton was assisted by a few other people who manned various machines. There was a TV screen which showed what was happening, and another monitoring my heart. As we proceeded I asked questions. I had already told Dr Sutton that I wished to be totally involved.

He inserted three wires into my thigh which were threaded up to my heart. Each section of my heart was tested, with the wires placed in different positions. It was made to beat from eighty to two hundred beats a minute for one minute at a time, bringing in one extra beat and then two. At one point he announced, 'There's no extra bundle.'

'No extra bundle,' I repeated, and felt glad.

After about an hour he appeared to have spotted something. 'What is it?' I asked anxiously.

'We have found an abnormal heart rhythm,' he replied—ventricular fibrillation.'

'Are you actually saying that you have found it?' I said excitedly. 'If so, I want to savour this moment, because I've waited twenty-three years for this!'

I knew that ventricular fibrillation usually leads to imminent cardiac arrest unless a defibrillator is at hand. And suddenly it all made sense, if that was what had happened to them all. I was sure that we had found the key.

Dr Sutton finished the tests and I was so grateful to him. 'What now?' I enquired as they prepared to wheel me back to the ward.

'You will be put on a drip immediately for twenty-four hours, which will pump a drug into you. Then you will take it in tablet form for the rest of your life.'

'What are the side-effects?' I asked as my head was disappearing around the door.

'Very rare,' he replied.

My excitement mounted as I neared the ward. It was two o'clock, visiting time. John might be there.

'They've found it! They've found it!' I shouted as I was wheeled in, and suddenly I was crying. Sheila came and held my hand tightly. 'Thank goodness!' she exclaimed, and the tears started rolling down her face too.

The nurses were overjoyed, and everyone was sharing in my relief, and then suddenly I saw John hurrying towards me. 'Darling, they've found something!' I cried out.

'Thank God!' he cried, taking me in his arms. 'Are you all right?'

'I'm fine,' I answered smiling, 'except that I'm starving. I haven't eaten or drunk a thing since six o'clock this morning!'

'I'll get you anything you want,' said a nurse, overhearing us.

'Right!' I exclaimed, feeling like a queen. 'I'll have a cup of tea, please, a boiled egg, and two pieces of toast.'

Soon after that a doctor came to put the drip in for me. It was while I was on this that Sheila decided that she wanted me to lay hands on her ankles, which were swollen. 'Well, you'll have to come nearer me,' I giggled, 'because I can't move with this thing on.' She came and placed her feet up on an armchair next to my bed, and somehow I laid hands on her ankles. The Lord's power came upon me strongly, so much so that it took my breath away, and the nurse asked me if I was all right!

During the following few days I felt very rough indeed. I was also in some conflict. I knew that the tests had not been available when the first three had died, but what about Rosemary? Could she have been saved? After thinking long and hard about it I came to the conclusion that events could not have happened in any other way. But now, if the others could be tested and nothing should be found, we could live in peace. If something should be found, we knew that it could be treated.

When the Senior Registrar, Dr Fitzpatrick, did his rounds, he gave me dates for the rest of the family to have tests.

'The words "thank you" seem inadequate to express what I feel,' I said.

The tall handsome doctor sat on the bed opposite me, and said with some desperation, 'We need money. The cardiac unit is under threat of closure. We have two operating theatres lying idle. We need thousands of pounds for new machinery and for research.'

My eyes lit up. 'I shall use our unique story to give you publicity,' I assured him.

When I left the hospital the story was featured in the press, on radio and television, but there is still a desperate need at Westminster Hospital for more funds.

In the weeks that followed, my brother and two sisters were tested, and so were Stephen (aged twenty-one) and Paul (eighteen). None of them was found to have the condition.

Not long afterwards John and I were strolling hand in hand along the river bank in the spring sunshine. On the opposite side some children were fishing. A swan glided silently across the water, followed by its family. A gentle breeze swept some blossom off the trees, and it fell like snowflakes around us.

I looked up, and took a deep breath. 'Oh, I'm so glad to be alive!'

'Thank God you *are* alive!' said John softly. 'How do you

feel, now that it's all over?'

I was silent for a moment.

'My feelings are still very mixed,' I sighed. 'There will always be sadness, but now that the mystery is solved it's like a burden's been lifted.'

We stopped, and John took both my hands in his.

'The Lord has used you so much already,' he said tenderly, 'but there must be thousands more who need your hands to touch them.'

I smiled before replying. 'And thousands more who need you to teach and train them.'

'I *do* love you, darling,' he said.

'I love you too, very much.'

We walked on, and my thoughts turned to a card which Mark and Lynda had given us. Underneath a picture of a golden key are the words from Jeremiah 29:11 (NIV):

'"For I know the plans I have for you," declares the Lord…"plans to give you hope and a future."'

Epilogue: To Those Who Would Heal

While we were writing this book the British Medical Association began a nationwide investigation into what it called 'alternative therapies'. Those responsible wanted to know which therapies were in use, and the conclusions of those practising them on how they worked.

We have never before summarized our 'methods of treatment', but John collected the information together and sent it to the B.M.A.

Stressing that we prefer to call what we minister *Christian* healing as opposed to *faith* healing, he explained that we see our work as complementary to that of the medical profession and wherever possible we encourage 'patients' who believe that they are cured to have this confirmed by their general practitioner. John added that we are also involved in training people in the ministry of healing and that we minister to the whole person: body, mind and spirit.

The following are the methods that we use, and we include them here in the hope that they will be of some help to those who would heal. At our training days and conferences John goes into much greater detail about the practicalities of how to apply them.

Laying on of hands

We believe that this works through a transference of healing energy from God to the person in need. This energy is transmitted through the hands of the healer, but it is not a mechanical process. Success may be hindered by resistance, tension or negative attitudes in either the sufferer or the healer. Jesus Christ promised that, besides doctors and gifted people, all believers in him could see the sick recover if they used this form of treatment (Mark 16:17–18).

We use laying on of hands at communion and healing services, but also in very informal contexts, where we believe that the power of touch adds to the effectiveness of spoken prayer. We sometimes accompany it by anointing the sick person with oil, a Christian symbol of healing in the power of the Holy Spirit.

Soaking prayer

When a sufferer shows signs of improvement after one or two sessions of laying on of hands we have often found it beneficial to provide a course of treatment in relaxed surroundings. We keep our hands on the affected part(s) of a person's body for long periods at a time—say twenty to thirty minutes—while we pray, worship in song, or talk informally. The energy flows through at the point of contact, but other areas of the body or personality may also derive benefit.

Positive thinking

We have found that negative words, thoughts and attitudes tend to restrict healing. We endeavour to picture the sufferer in a healthy condition—for example, the crippled walking or the blind seeing—while praying positively, specifically and expectantly though without giving false hopes.

Whenever possible we attempt to discover the root cause(s) of the person's physical problems, which often lie in the mental or emotional realm. We believe that Jesus Christ can go back in time to the point where a disease was first contracted and we encourage the 'patient' to imagine Jesus there, putting things right. The result has frequently been an inner freedom and a consequent physical healing. Painful traumas of the past hurt the person no more and in Jesus' name we minister to him positive virtues like love, peace and strength.

Prayer counselling

This is a kind of Christian psychiatry for which we have been trained, though we ourselves no longer do much of it as John is training others to minister it. It involves spending a long period (say two hours) listening to a person in need as he shares things which are most worrying him and talks about any unhappy childhood experiences or traumas of the past which have badly affected him.

We then lay hands on him and pray at length about each matter as the Holy Spirit leads us. In the course of this there may be prayer and ministry for physical or mental affliction; deliverance from harmful bondages; healing of memories, hurts and wounds; confession of sin and spoken forgiveness to aid the healing of relationships; and equipping for Christian service.

God puts words or pictures into our minds, which when shared, act as a trigger to the person's memory, bring to light the most necessary areas for 'treatment'. These can then be ministered to specifically. We don't normally give advice, but God may speak through us to the sufferer in prophecy or by other charismatic gifts (see 1 Corinthians 12:8–10).

The spoken word

This can be very effective, especially when used alongside other methods of healing.

We not only use 'request' prayers but 'command' ones— for example, 'In the name of Jesus, be healed!' or 'Rise up and walk!' We also believe that united prayer can release healing energy. And when a sick person is unable to be present we have nevertheless found that our prayers avail for him. Someone may stand in proxy for him for the laying on of hands, just as the centurion came to Jesus for his slave who was ill at home (Matthew 8:6–13).

When a person is psychologically bound in a harmful way to his sickness, or to a person, attitude, addiction, etc., we speak the authoritative word of God (or read it from the Scriptures). This we believe is the sword of the Holy Spirit, and we use it to cut through the invisible chains and set the person free at a deep level.

If he is in the grip of evil forces (but not necessarily mentally ill) we minister deliverance and if necessary exorcism. The latter we believe should only be performed by trained and experienced Christians because of the possible dangers involved. But, provided that proper after-care is given, after this sort of ministry there is invariably transformation in the person concerned.

Encouragement to respond and to lead a balanced life

Alongside all the other means of healing that we use, we encourage the sufferer to consult his G.P. when necessary and to act as far as he is able on what has been ministered. Every case is different and there is much that we don't understand, but we believe that if all the right facilities are present a cure can be effected.

In Christian terms faith is a necessary requirement, and the person in need must himself have faith in Christ for healing of spirit. For healing of body or mind he may be cured without having faith himself, but it is necessary for someone to have faith if prayer is used. Unbelief, resentment or lack of released power are other hindrances to healing by these methods, and the atmosphere in which the 'treatment' is given is important—be it in church, home or hospital.

While we have had some instances of healing (including instantaneous ones) where no medical treatment has been used, most cures appear to be effected by a combination of means. So we encourage those who ask us for ministry to make use of every good means available for acquiring and maintaining health and fitness. This includes lifestyle, prayer, sacrament, medicine, environment, diet, exercise, and everything else that makes for wholeness.